AD

"*Don't Panic!* can help each of us cope with the ups and downs of life, by getting in touch with the Spirit within and by using mindful breathing, prayers, and letting this grace-filled book be your guide. *Don't Panic!* can transform you and your life from the inside out."

—CHERYL WUNSCH, MEd, RNCS, clinical nurse specialist and psychotherapist in private practice

"Maureen knows pain. She knows chronic illness and the isolation that comes with it, the feelings of abandonment and all the related emotional responses. However, as a woman of faith, she also understands that suffering can be a way to unite with Jesus, our suffering Savior. As a prayerful woman, she understands the spiritual medicine that is available to us through our conversations with the Lord. As a member of CUSA, an apostolate of persons with chronic illness and disability, she also knows the need for support from others. She offers her support through her writing apostolate as well as through her lectures. This latest effort is another in the library of wisdom that she has offered us, wisdom that is a product of her life of prayer and ministry to others."

—FR. LAWRENCE JAGDFELD, OFM, administrator, CUSA, an Apostolate of Persons with Chronic Illness or Disability (www.cusan.org)

"To those in crisis, to those who fear, to those who love, Maureen Pratt speaks from deep reservoirs of prayer and tender intimacy with pain. She leads us through the fire and calls us to pray, laugh, cry, reach out, choose, reflect, and pray some more. A guidebook for all of us who travel on the precarious road of life."

—BETSEY BECKMAN, founder, The Dancing Word (www.thedancingword.com)

"In *Don't Panic!* Maureen Pratt offers a beautifully written and much appreciated consoling voice that integrates spiritual, psychological, relational, and behavioral insights to help those who are struggling and may be in the dark night of the soul. She journeys with the reader as a spiritual friend and trusted mentor. Her compelling book will be a cool and refreshing drink for the thirsty reader."

—THOMAS G. PLANTE, PhD, ABPP is the Augustin Cardinal Bea, S.J. University Professor and Director of the Spirituality and Health Institute at Santa Clara University

"Maureen Pratt is an inspiring writer who goes when the going is tough! Whenever I feel that I have it tough, I consider people like Maureen, who keep their cool in spite of adversity and fearlessly strive for life's best. Whether reporting someone else's, or sharing her own wisdom, she never fails to deliver!"

—JOHN FEISTER, editor in chief, *St. Anthony Messenger* magazine

"This is not just another self-help book. Drawing on a deepening spirituality in dealing with hcr own life-shattering crises, Maureen Pratt focuses on how she's lived her ordinary life, centered on an awareness of God's active presence, and how it has prepared her to survive and thrive in the midst of crisis. Learning from her wisdom and experience is something like fastening your seatbelt when driving. You may ordinarily get by without it, but when you need it, it can mean the difference between life and death. Maureen's is a wonderful story that we all can enjoy and take to heart."

—FR. TOM WELBERS, a retired priest in the archdiocese of Los Angeles

"*Don't Panic!* is the perfect name for a book so needed today. Maureen Pratt has a lovely and soothing writing voice that instills encouragement, faith-filled hope, and practical ways to manage the intense stresses we face. Are you having a tough time? You'll be glad you picked up this book!"

—ANGELA BREIDENBACH, president, Christian Authors Network

HOW TO
KEEP GOING
WHEN THE GOING
GETS TOUGH

DON'T PANIC!

MAUREEN PRATT

Franciscan
MEDIA
Cincinnati, Ohio

Cover design by LUCAS Art & Design
Book design by Mark Sullivan

LIBRARY OF CONGRESS CATALOGING-IN-PUBLICATION DATA
Names: Pratt, Maureen, author.
Title: Don't panic! : how to keep going when the going gets tough / Maureen Pratt.
Description: Cincinnati : Franciscan Media, 2016. | Includes bibliographical references.
Identifiers: LCCN 2016002484 | ISBN 9781616369491
Subjects: LCSH: Anxiety—Religious aspects—Christianity.
Stress (Psychology)—Religious aspects—Christianity.
Classification: LCC BV4908.5 .P73 2016 | DDC 248.8/6--dc23
LC record available at http://lccn.loc.gov/2016002484

ISBN 978-1-61636-949-1

Published by Franciscan Media
28 W. Liberty St.
Cincinnati, OH 45202
www.FranciscanMedia.org

Printed in the United States of America.
Printed on acid-free paper.
16 17 18 19 20   5 4 3 2 1

CONTENTS

"These are the times that try men's souls."
—Thomas Paine, *The Crisis*, December 23, 1776

Perhaps history does not repeat itself completely, but many times, someone's words written centuries ago sound as if they could have been written today. Revolutionary War patriot Thomas Paine might have been referring to life in eighteenth-century America, but I can certainly relate to the feeling of his statement, and I'm sure I'm not alone. Like many, I've lived through more than one trying time. Whether brought on by natural disasters, accidents, or more personal catalysts, these life-changing (and sometimes life-shattering) events can truly shake our lives and souls to their very core, and bring fresh and deep hurt that can linger for a long time. Crises can also color how we look at the future, making us warier of change and fearful of the unknown.

But however negative they may be, crises can also be positive. They can strengthen us, bond us more tightly with loved ones, reveal talents we did not realize we had, teach us about skillful and healthful coping, and give us a greater appreciation for this world and this life. If we had faith before, crises can put our faith into blessed action, increasing our belief and reliance upon God, and give us extra support, especially when the situation is bleakest. Likewise, many who might not believe in God before a crisis often discover a depth of Spirit and ability that transcends their own limited human capacity to cope without it.

It is this revelation of the power of the Spirit in a crisis that is truly one of the most positive aspects of living with and through adversity.

Far from being naïve, this aspect of crisis is a profound blessing, but often overlooked in the face of the visceral power of images and feelings that convey fear, violence, loss, and pain. Especially today, when negative news seems utterly pervasive, we are consciously and subconsciously exposed to much more of the downside of disasters, personal or public, than any appreciable upside. We are encouraged, overtly and tacitly, to accept a much grimmer reality than there truly is.

• • •

My first experience with a real crisis showed me just how important spiritual supports are, and how even the bleakest events need not be crushingly disastrous.

I grew up in the tornado-prone Midwest. One night, I remember being lifted out of bed by my father and carried downstairs, right behind my mother, who had my brother in tow. Moments earlier, she had felt the wind push in heavily the bedroom wall. She knew that a tornado was coming, and so she and my father took me and my brother downstairs to safety.

What a wild yet surprisingly peaceful night! I was about nine years old, and my brother was about five. We were sleepy and a bit confused, but we were not afraid as our parents calmly settled us in the basement and pulled out toys, blankets, and flashlights. Huddled together, as the wind and rain raged outside and lightning punctuated the shadows, we played and prayed and finally fell asleep, not knowing that two powerful tornadoes were bearing down on our community.

I don't remember the storms ending, but the next day, we woke to sun-drenched warmth. Birds sang as if nothing horrible had happened the night before. It seemed a beautiful day for a walk, but as soon as we went outside, the scene was marred by ugliness.

As if a random, angry fist had come down from the sky the night before, we walked past one house standing, intact, and another flattened to the ground. We passed by front yards churned as if having been plowed for spring crops, and front yards where trees stood firm and spring flowers bloomed, unbowed by the storms that had passed.

We stopped to talk with a neighbor who lived across the street. He told us he had watched as one of the funnel clouds hovered over our house, but did not touch down. His house was all right, too, but the one next to his had been obliterated, except for the chimney. I learned later that the first tornado had been an EF-1, relatively mild, but the second one had been an EF-4, one notch below the EF-5 tornado that devastated Joplin, Missouri, in May 2011!

Besides the visual devastation, I remember how people seemed to react differently to the tornadoes' impact. Some moved mechanically through the remains of their homes, stooped over as they looked for anything they could save. Some people were angry; you could hear it in their voices and see it in their clenched jaws and fists. Other people seemed to not be as bothered, but were already digging in, shovel or broom in hand. Still others found humor, chuckling at the rumor that the roof of someone's house had been blown off, and a woman in bed was picked up, thrown into a front yard several houses away, and still survived without injury. (I don't know if this was true; in crises, there are often stories that swirl around with the facts, getting tangled in the "news," so it's hard to pull truth from fiction.)

Neighbors whose homes had not sustained much or any damage reached out to those who were less fortunate. Cleanup commenced in earnest.

I suppose some psychologists would say that I should have suffered tremendous trauma by viewing the damage in my neighborhood, but I felt no fear or panic moving through the community, nor did I feel it inside my young heart. Of course, at that time, I couldn't comprehend the entirety of what those tornadoes had done. After all, my family and I were safe, and our house was intact.

I don't think my resilience was due only to my young age and the relatively good outcome for my family that stormy night. The calm exhibited by my parents when they carried me and my brother downstairs had assured me right from the start. They had prepared us by regularly doing tornado drills with us, and they stored familiar things in the basement in case we ever had to hunker down there. They prayed with us, too, so we had a sense of protection beyond the walls of our house. With all the preparation and the steadfast attitude communicated by my parents, I felt that, no matter what was going to happen, my life was going to be OK.

As for the feeling in the neighborhood, beyond my family, looking back, I think that perhaps there was no anger (against the tornadoes or the neighbors who were spared) or panic in the aftermath because there was an understanding: Tornadoes are a fact of life in the Midwest. Moreover, no matter who you are or where you live, crises—accidents, disasters, and other negative events—will inevitably happen.

What matters is how you respond to them—before, during, and after.

Those lessons of preparation, coping skills, and spiritual stability served as a firm foundation for my reaction to every danger and every negative event to come. I don't always sail through adversity. There have been plenty of bumps along the road and times when I could have responded better earlier on in the crisis. But inevitably the result from any adverse event, however negative, has yielded positive effects, too.

Crises do strengthen us. When we look back on how we got through them, they do give us greater courage. And above all, they enable us to witness how the Spirit works no matter what might be falling apart around us, and this is immensely comforting—a tremendous antidote to panic!

Life Rolling Along, and Then…

My definition of what a crisis is can be distilled to a precipitating or ongoing negative event that may impact us either directly or indirectly and that causes us pain or trauma that turns our normal lives upside down, throwing us into uncertainty or confusion. In our daily lives, it might begin with the telephone ringing, the earth rumbling, or a tornado's freight-train-like sound pushing against the walls of our homes.

A crisis might start with someone whispering, "We have to talk," or begin when your doctor's eyes don't quite meet yours as you come into the examination room for test results.

Besides these kinds of crises, spiritual or personal crises occur sometimes, too. These might begin more subtly and build over time, perhaps starting with a feeling that something in your life is horribly askew, a darkness descending over your heart and the world in which you move, work, and love. As you become more covered by this cloud of darkness, you might feel more hopeless, as if even the slightest problem compounds the feeling that life is moving in a terribly negative direction.

Whether you are faced with external tragedy or loss, or an internal, growing sense of displacement and hopelessness, in a crisis, your life is changed as if the before-now solid ground beneath your feet is shifting, and stability and control vanish.

As I witnessed in the tornadic aftermath in my neighborhood, people react differently to a crisis. Some freeze and others stir themselves into a frenzy of activity. Some have a strong, internal sense, a deep faith, that all will be well no matter what is happening—and no matter how much life changes in the aftermath. Others immediately go from crisis to doom, and let that dour prognosis color their thoughts, feelings, and actions for a long time, perhaps a lifetime, afterward.

There's no doubt that sudden or gradually building negative events can create havoc in our physical world. A car accident can physically render us as an almost-stranger to ourselves. A chronic illness can create built-up stress that festers, exacerbating already-painful symptoms. Crises can cost us our jobs, money, and other material possessions. They can tear families and communities apart by obliterating people, buildings, and infrastructure.

But perhaps more impactful is the toll crises have on our oh-so-vulnerable human hearts. Whether at midlife, retirement, or earlier, in those formative and turbulent teenage years, crises can prompt questions about mortality, God, purpose, commitment, and truth that can set our heads spinning and our footsteps on rocky and unsettling paths. We might doubt all that we've known to be true, including who we are and what our place in the world is.

And it's not just the crises themselves that can bring on this very bleak worldview. No, it's ordinary, everyday, twenty-first-century life!

"The Times That Try Men's (and Women's) Souls"

Think about what frightens you today, and you'll probably come up with a rather long list. Fear is all around us and very often in us in today's world, especially fear of what *might* happen. With each natural disaster, incident of local violence, or personal loss, our internal fear sensor is given more kindling for its fire. We might be sitting on our comfy sofas or walking through a peaceful forest, and we still might be filled with anxiety! Think about it, when was the last time you said, "What if something bad happens?" or "What if the news is bad?" or merely "What if…" with a glance behind you to see if anything was lurking there?

Each time we think something like that, or say it, or engage in an entire conversation focused on it, we're expressing the anxiety within us. And that anxiety is feeding a well of stress, which in turn bubbles up to create more anxiety.

To protect ourselves from dreaded, perceived, or real threats, we might take tangible precautions. We lock our doors, buy insurance, stockpile survival supplies, plan an escape route, or adopt a really big, loud dog.

To stave off health crises, we throw ourselves into a frenzy of exercise (at least for a time), and we throw our money into buying expensive dietary supplements.

To avoid personal crises, we might jump through myriad hoops to vet a future spouse, a company we might work for, or a community we might move to.

Many of these actions are prudent or necessary for us to be healthfully, physically prepared and protected. It is good to do what we can to take care of ourselves, our families, and our communities. But even with all of those, and sometimes more, precautions to protect ourselves, we might still be anxious or even panicky, especially if something goes bump in the night. Why?

We are exposed to external pressure on a daily basis. This pressure promotes a constant state of imbalance—more dread than security. From stark pictures of war, famine, and other worldwide problems, we are exposed daily, even hourly, to a visual, audible presence of upsetting, upending trouble in our world. And in our own neighborhoods, the rumor mill delights in churning out the latest and goriest details of this or that private disaster, passed on by that one gossipy person each of us knows.

Moreover, even seemingly innocuous reportage adds to this underlying stress-building action. So-called authoritative surveys or reports often point out potential crises-in-the-making very close to or even at home. For example, "Most car accidents happen within blocks of one's home," or, "Most emergency room visits are because of at-home accidents!" Or there might be an emphasis on all the diseases and health conditions you *might* suffer from, and all the awful side-effects you *might* get by taking medication for those awful conditions. Then, of course, there are those cyber threats that lurk behind every email, photo attachment, or website visit.

We not only get negative, stress-building images and messages from external sources, but often we bring them on ourselves. A steady exposure to people or situations that disrespect and denigrate you or others can leave you feeling skittish, debased, and victimized. A steady diet of violent films, games, or music can make these seem commonplace, and that which is good, beautiful, and grace-filled might begin to seem uncomfortably foreign.

These are only a few of the negative influences around us that, day in and day out, chip away at our resilience and ability to hear and heed the wisdom within our souls and find peace. They obscure goodness and hope and promote fear and negativity.

Yes, it is easy to get spiritual indigestion as we navigate our lives through this all too modern world! But it is also possible and, often, easy to moderate our diet of these stress builders!

Through the many crises I've endured, whether accidents, acts of nature, or deeply personal life experiences, I've learned that we need not panic in the face of today's world or today's crises, and we need not be victims to the forces that prey upon our spiritual well-being. We have many internal resources, some we already know about and some that are largely undeveloped and untapped that include creativity, adaptability, foresight, and compassion. These are not necessarily skills we could point to on our resumes for a job interview, but they are personal qualities given to us directly from our Creator. If they are well-nurtured and properly employed, they enable us to be stable when we are shaken and be safe when we are singed.

When Thomas Paine wrote his famous tract *The Crisis,* the Age of Enlightenment, with its emphasis on science and reason, was sweeping across Europe and influencing many of the leaders in colonial America who used some religiously associated words and concepts without meaning them to be construed in a specific, doctrinal context. Thus, the word *soul* in Paine's worldview might today be more akin to our use of the words *heart* or *good spirit.*

In this book, I use the word *soul* to mean the God-created spiritual essence of each individual. *Spirit* (capital *S*) is the God-bestowed, holy gift that animates us as creative, loving, compassionate people and that supports us to have the spirit (small *s*), will, or heart to persevere, make good decisions, and pursue and nurture spiritual strength and resilience.

In other words: We people, body and soul, have a Spirit that infuses us with God's love and light, and our willingness, heart, and spirit to nurture our relationship with that Spirit, and thus God, enables us to develop tremendous spiritual resilience and strength in and apart from crises.

Of course, developing strong spiritual coping skills takes time, much like exercise builds stamina and flexibility. But as I've consciously worked on my inner spiritual life, external problems both large and small have become more manageable and, blessedly, never hopeless. Moreover, God is not a concept or a bearded man sitting in eternal judgment, but rather a powerful support in and through every aspect of life. And my openness to accepting the harshest circumstances, the murkiest of crises, has enabled me to reap blessings beyond anything I'd ever imagined possible.

Despite what others offer—people, advertisements, news stories, or rumor—we do not have to take on the cloak of victim. We do not have to crumble under the weight of adversity.

We do not have to panic. But we can all use a bit more (or a lot more) strength and courage. And that is why I wrote this book.

What You'll Find Here

Within these pages are stories and science, challenges and validations for navigating life today with less fear, more positive energy, and a stronger spirit. These are things I've found important in facing my own crises, including catastrophic health problems, natural disasters (besides the tornadoes), accidents, and personal upheaval. There are also things that I've learned from others, whether they lived long ago or are still alive today—canonized saints and unsung saints who live among us, human beings like you and me who, when confronted with awful events, managed to rise above in amazing and inspiring ways. Some of the people I mention in this book will be familiar to you, and others will be strangers. My aim is not to put these people up on pedestals, but to illustrate *how* they did it, emphasizing the tools they used to rise to challenges, tools that we also possess in abundance.

As a longtime health journalist, I have reported many times on areas of mind-body medicine, a field that is growing by the day and promises to shed quantifiable light on the connections between the physical "us" and the spiritual "us." Not long ago, when I began writing about health-related and spiritual topics, many physicians and other medical professionals were not open to discussing these topics, let alone to pouring research efforts and hours into exploring them.

Now, with areas such as resilience training, and institutes of spirituality and health affiliated with major medical centers, and the inclusion of spirituality as a component of medical training, the tension between health science and spirituality is easing to form more positively curious and open-minded discussions. Some intriguing examples of this are included here via interviews and analyses of already-published studies. Through them, I hope to highlight ways we can understand ourselves better through some of the mind-body techniques that are readily available to us, extremely useful tools for good times and bad, especially if folded into a regular practice or routine.

I will also explore the deep connection and conversation between faith and Spirit. Faith plays a crucial role in my life, whether in calm or turmoil. But it is not as simple as saying, "I have faith." Instead, for me, faith is the open door to trust and spiritual presence in many different aspects of living.

First, I have faith in God. It might not always be easy for me to understand or accept God's purpose in a crisis, but faith in his presence and trust in his care throughout makes those trying times bountifully blessed and allows me to find spiritual calm when all else is in turmoil.

My faith in God finds tangible expression in the Roman Catholic Church. There, worship and a faith community have a central place in my cultivation of spiritual strength and heart. This is a blessing to me in overt, as well as deeply personal, ways and brings joy, support, insight, and much humor to me daily.

But, my faith also goes beyond the walls of the church and touches every other aspect of life. Firmly linked with another word, *trust*, faith allows me to build strength in areas that are important for supporting serenity, healthful relationships, and a better ability to bounce back when difficult times press down hard. For example, I have faith in the good people in my life, I trust them to behave in honorable ways toward and for me in times of crises (for example, if I needed them to make medical decisions for me when I could not do so myself). This faith and trust allow me to feel less anxious if I think of the possibility of my lupus flaring unexpectedly, or if any other crisis arises. They fuel personal growth!

You'll find sections called "Faith in Focus." These are starting points to help you think of the specific people, crises, and other parts of your life when you've had to call upon faith, trust, and other resources to get through a difficult period or problem. The scenarios and questions are meant to encourage you to see how, in these individual events and with these individual people, your faith played a key role, and because of this, the future can also be enhanced and more secure.

The exercises should also help you better articulate and benefit from the direct connection between your faith and the security of your spiritual well-being. I realize we are all on individual journeys of faith; some people believe deeply, others are less sure, and still others, at least at the present time, might reject faith. Perhaps this is you; you don't quite know what to believe, or you find it hard to believe because you cannot touch, see, or otherwise concretely know God, and the reality of the Spirit is too elusive—you will believe only what you perceive as true.

I believe in living truthfully; however, my sense is different from those who reject faith: I believe that we isolate ourselves from being fully, truly human, and away from one another, when we deny the depth of Spirit within us and the role of faith that connects us to ourselves, each other, and God. We are more than reactive beings, victims of every circumstance, especially crises, and it is the Spirit that ignites us to be active, feel secure, and come through resiliently. And it is acknowledgment of the presence of God that brings us profound security always, especially when we're most shaken.

So for me, the only true way to live is with full engagement of all of who we are—body, mind, emotion, and Spirit. Not that we do or say anything we want, whenever we want; this only leads to more unhappiness, confusion, and panic. For me, the only way to feel even and whole in this life is to strive for stability in all four of those areas. So as we recognize our complete human condition, learning all we can so that we are aware of how these seeming separate areas work together, we find more strength in taking good care of all we are. The "Faith in Focus" sections will also, I hope, help you develop your own faith and Spirit vocabulary and better recognize where these two essential elements work in your life.

Prayer is vital to my entire life, but especially to keeping my communication with God and the Spirit moving. A chapter on prayer talks about the emerging scientific awareness of the intersection of prayer and health, and different styles and forms of prayer, as well as suggestions for building a mightier muscle when it comes to tuning out distractions and tuning in to God.

Finally, I hope that as you read, you'll say, at least once, "Well, I could have told you that," or, "I already do that." This validation isn't for my benefit, but it's important because we often forget how many resources we have close at hand to grow stronger and more resilient. These validations are touchstones to remind us of the courage that's already within our souls, the hero, indeed inside. And as we remember what we already have done, the times when we haven't panicked but have acted with courage and strength, we will be better equipped to believe and act even more impactfully the next time a crisis occurs.

There is a tremendous hero inside each of us, a person who can face a crisis and bring to bear inner strength, vitality, courage, and compassion. As you appreciate and develop the heroic qualities within you that protect you and your loved ones from darkness and allow the Spirit to thrive, I hope you will begin to trust even more firmly that, no matter what, there is no need to panic. There is great reason to have faith, hope, and love.

CHAPTER ONE

Who Are You in a Crisis?

"I praise you because I am fearfully and wonderfully made."
—Psalm 139:14 (New International Version)

The New American Bible's translation of this verse from Psalm 139 is slightly different. It reads, "I praise you; so wonderfully you made me; wonderful are your works!" But I chose to use the translation from the NIV because, when it comes to crises, we often do seem to be "fearfully and wonderfully" made as our bodies, minds, and emotions react and interact to crises.

I especially remember one period when life erupted into several crises, and my physical and emotional reactions challenged my ability to cope.

Nearly eighteen years ago, lupus was threatening my life. I was on heavy immunosuppressive drugs, including one usually used for chemotherapy and one potent steroid. I couldn't work, my physical appearance had changed radically because I lost all of my hair and had noticeable lupus rashes, and my life's purpose was unclear, at best. Relationships were falling away as my illness took deeper hold. Then, my brother, my only sibling, died suddenly. He had just turned thirty-four.

When I hung up the phone after hearing the news from my mother, I paced through my apartment, gasping for air. I reached out at nothing, as if I could pull back time and pull back my brother. I kept praying, "Lord, this can't be happening. Not my brother. Not now."

My grief was compounded when I checked my emails later that day and saw one in my inbox from him, sent within hours of his death. It was a silly e-mail; nothing in it indicated he would soon die. But it, too, added pain upon pain as I realized so very tangibly the fleetingness of time and the suddenness of irreversible change.

For days, I couldn't sleep more than a little at a time. The weight of emotional shock and physical burdens was heavy. My prayer life became a lifeline, a way to keep close to God and cling to his hope and comfort. But still, I would have become absolutely overwhelmed if it had not been for the support of my mother, good friends, and church family.

At the time, I was conducting an African American gospel choir at a Catholic church in Southern California. Upon hearing what was going on, my choir family stepped up. One member drove me to Mass; another drove me home. They prayed over me and over my mother and the entire situation. They checked in on me and encouraged me in myriad ways. It was tangible faith in action.

Through the days that followed, I was able to take care of necessary phone calls and other responsibilities, such as notifying my doctors so they could change or tweak my medications in light of the extra stress that had fallen. I can't say I was being particularly brave, but I was relying heavily on God, praying for wisdom, strength, and guidance as the questions hit me hard:

How had my brother died? The circumstances were unclear.

When would the memorial service be held, and would I be able to travel to get there? My health and emotional state were beyond fragile.

What would be the long-term effects of this stress on my illness? How would I be able to cope with more medical challenges when I had so many already?

How long would it take to get over this trauma, this pain?

It helped to write down my questions and rambling thoughts, sometimes in a formal prayer journal and other times on whatever bits of paper were at hand. I tried to be quiet and listen for God's replies, but this was a very roiled time. Sometimes, it was impossible to feel I was getting anywhere with my prayers; my mind and heart were too overloaded. Sometimes, all I heard was the hard beating of my heart, and nothing spiritual could come through. Other times, I heard answers but they weren't easy to take; God was leading me through the pain, not taking it away.

Up to this point, I had developed some strong prayer muscles during other crises and in calmer times. I had experienced long stretches before when God's voice was difficult to discern, or when his answer was not, "I will lift this burden," but rather, "I will help you carry it." In those times, I knew to give myself enough variety of prayer, place, and manner, to finally connect. (I'll go into more detail about this in chapter seven.) I also consciously avoided becoming angry with God, angry with the pain of loss and illness; I knew from seeing others become consumed with anger that it did nothing positive and only sapped more energy from already broken hearts. I fully accepted that sometimes we will hurt, be ill, endure hardships—these are not bad or evil, they just are. The point is how we react through them.

As the events unfolded and as I kept praying, my upended life righted itself. Relying upon God, my loved ones, and a great variety of other coping resources, slowly, I began to heal.

"Wonderfully and Fearfully Made"

Individuals' reactions to crises are as old as history itself. Consider this description of the chaos during the devastating volcanic eruption of Mt. Vesuvius in August 79 BC, which obliterated the city of Pompeii and other nearby towns. Written by eighteen-year-old Pliny the Younger, who fled the city of Misenum (today's Miseno) with his mother, the words have an eerily contemporary feel:

Ashes were already falling, not as yet very thickly. I looked round: a dense black cloud was coming up behind us, spreading over the earth like a flood. "Let us leave the road while we can still see," I said, "or we shall be knocked down and trampled underfoot in the dark by the crowd behind." We had scarcely sat down to rest when darkness fell, not the dark of a moonless or cloudy night, but as if the lamp had been put out in a closed room.

You could hear the shrieks of women, the wailing of infants, and the shouting of men; some were calling their parents, others their children or their wives, trying to recognize them by their voices. People bewailed their own fate or that of their relatives, and there were some who prayed for death in their terror of dying. Many besought the aid of the gods, but still more imagined there were no gods left, and that the universe was plunged into eternal darkness for evermore.

There were people, too, who added to the real perils by inventing fictitious dangers: some reported that part of Misenum had collapsed or another part was on fire, and though their tales were false, they found others to believe them. A gleam of light returned, but we took this to be a warning of the approaching flames rather than daylight. However, the flames remained some distance off; then darkness came on once more and ashes began to fall again, this time in heavy showers. We rose from time to time and shook them off, otherwise we should have been buried and crushed beneath their weight. I could boast that not a groan or cry of fear escaped me in these perils, but I admit that I derived some poor consolation in my mortal lot from the belief that the whole world was dying with me and I with it.[1]

Pliny's words were written in a letter to a friend several years after the disaster; by fleeing when and how he and his mother did, they survived. So, despite his seeming resigned attitude (the "belief that the whole world was dying with" him), Pliny forged ahead, astutely noticing how best to move and how to avoid the pitfalls of being trapped or trampled by a large, frightened crowd!

This is a tremendous example of an inner Spirit that insists on living and an inner perception that knew how to do just that. It also shows how the Spirit transcends instinct; if he had been reacting from merely a desire to save himself (instinct alone), Pliny the Younger would have left his less-abled mother far behind.

You have probably heard of the phrase "fight or flight," a description of the instinctive reactions people have to accidents, disasters, or other crises. Behavior experts believe that these feelings and the actions they precipitate are deeply ingrained in our being; a powerful residual from days when civilization was not so civilized, and there were many more serious threats in everyday life.[2] These instincts are not necessarily carved in stone; spiritual practice and faith (for example, the blessing and virtue of forgiving someone who has grievously wounded us), as well as a growing body of scientific research, suggest we can retrain our minds and hearts and learn to act differently. But for now, I'll start with the basics.

In the physical sense, "fight" is much like "stand and punch back." For example, if someone wrongs us, we will fight back, or if the fire is rapidly approaching, we'll grab another hose and use both hands. Or someone will have a take charge attitude, immediately trying to organize, compartmentalize, and otherwise control the uncontrollable.

"Flight" can be as subtle as denial, "I'm sure things aren't all that bad," or, "I'll wake up and all this will have been a bad dream." When I was working on my book *Taking Charge of Lupus: How to Manage the Disease and Make the Most of Your Life*, I learned from my doctors (and firsthand experience) that denial is often a critical reaction to a lupus diagnosis (or any other serious illness). The disease is complex, some-times life-threatening, and most times it is too much for patients to digest all at once. Denial allows a patient to slowly take in all the pieces of the diagnosis, with the hope that he or she will be less traumatized in the long run.

The flight response can also be manifested in physically leaving the traumatizing (hurtful or painful) situation—a marriage is on the brink and one spouse takes off (takes flight), or work becomes intolerable and someone abruptly quits.

In reaction to sudden trauma some people might go into physical shock and require medical attention. Others might have abundant energy at first, and then collapse later. Still others might burst into tears and retreat from the situation if they can. Others might immediately turn to prayer. Still others might laugh hysterically, to the point of pain, and then stop, recover, and move ahead.

Would you be able to recognize shock? Would you know what to do? Here are some signs of shock.[3] If you or someone you know is having these symptoms and signs, call 911 to seek prompt medical care:

- Confusion or lack of alertness
- Loss of consciousness
- A sudden and ongoing rapid heartbeat
- Sweating
- Pale skin
- A weak pulse
- Rapid breathing
- Decreased or no urine output
- Cool hands and feet

Emotional reactions are often intricately intertwined with the physical reactions. When I heard the news about my brother's death, I didn't think about it, I just started pacing rapidly from one room to the next, trying to walk off the deep sense of anguish I felt. Other times, in the early moments of a devastating event, I have gone into shock— chilled to the bone in the middle of a heat wave, heart beating more than when I exercise.

Sometimes our actions seem out of character, not how we would normally behave. You might find you have to start walking—around the block or around the room—or collapse on a sofa or chair and stare into space. One time, a friend in the midst of a bad breakup, peeled all of the pink nail polish off her fingernails onto the living room floor, a very descriptive example of emotions channeled into unlikely activity. Not normal at all, and yet, the circumstances aren't normal, either.

Stereotypes of how a man or woman should behave in a crisis often fly in the face of what really happens. News outlets abound with unlikely stories: An elderly woman tackling an intruder, for example, or a brawny football player who cries on camera when talking about the death of a beloved coach. Yes, we are all unique!

• FAITH IN FOCUS •

Identify a crisis you've lived through already. How did you physically react at first? How did your reaction change as time passed? Write down everything you can remember about the situation and your reactions. What have you learned about yourself? Have faith that you can unlock the mystery of your reactions to crises.

_____

_____

_____

Man or woman, your physical reactions to crises are yours, part of your unique make-up. Of course, if they rise to violence against yourself or others, are unhealthful in some other way (binge drinking, smoking, engaging in other risky behavior), or are inappropriately expressed in front of those too young to understand, then the reaction is not right. Also, preexisting health conditions should not be ignored; it's important to seek medical help immediately if you feel your health is compromised, you or someone else might be going into shock, or you begin to experience new or recurring, troubling symptoms (such as a heart attack or stroke).

But the better you understand who you are in a crisis, the better your ability to handle all the necessary activities of coping *and* come through on firm footing.

Come through, how? Crying or raging like when the crisis began? Broken? Bowed down?

Probably not. Our initial reaction to extreme problems is usually nothing like how we will react the next day, or even a few hours after the phone rings or the car is towed away. Moreover, each crisis has a life, with a beginning, middle, and end (perhaps not finite, but at least a point at which life moves on), much like the landscape changing as we adapt, act, and assess our place in it.

This understanding of the life cycle of a crisis allowed me to move through the dark days after my brother's death with a deeper sense of support. I had faith that, as surely as prayer was a comfort and the sun rose each day, time would pass, and the acute stage of the crisis would fade. But I knew that to avoid becoming a victim to grief, I had to be active.

After the initial shock, I started to do all I could to support my health, gain clarity about the event itself, and make necessary arrangements. The mere act of doing my daily range of motion exercises helped, as did regular household errands and chores. Ordinary life can be a tremendous balm when extraordinarily difficult circumstances arise!

I couldn't travel immediately, but in a few weeks' time, and with my doctors' permission, I was able to go to Casey's funeral. It was one of the hardest things I've ever had to do, but the good that came of it outweighed the painful. I gained some closure; I was physically in a familiar, comforting place with family; and I learned I was strong enough to weather hardship with and in spite of my illness.

The night he was laid to rest, rolling thunder and crackling lightning tore through the stillness. In the storm's wake, there was peace and abundant new spiritual growth as I felt deep gratitude for his life and God's protective hand on me throughout the ordeal.

I look upon that night as a bookend to the time long ago when Casey and I were hunkered in the basement with our parents, tornadoes raging outside, and then, in the morning, there was utter calm. Underpinning the entire experience, God was with us, as he was with my mother and me when Casey died. And no matter what the storms brought, the Spirit dwelled peacefully and brought us back into the light of a new day.

There Are Crises and Then There Are Crises…

As we understand how we react to adverse situations, and as we navigate through them with more robust physical, emotional, and spiritual skills, we are better able to understand when a negative event merits the description "crisis," or when it is something of lesser weight. This is a wonderful thing to be able to do because it helps us lessen the extreme stress brought on by everyday life and concentrate our strength and efforts on tackling problems that are truly of consequence. It also helps us avoid placing inappropriate value on the little things that might seem like crises if our perspective is even a bit warped. Thus, a bad hair day or a lost shirt button might be hard to deal with, or humbling, but we will live, breathe, and move throughout the day without deep hurt! And although late-night infomercials ("Do you suffer from the pain of unwanted hair?") and larger-than-life billboards ("Your financial ruin could be just around the corner") encourage us to recognize less-certain or less-dire things as crises, they seldom are (although the financial ruin could result in calling the number on the advertisement).

The loss of a loved one, a tragic accident, sudden downsizing at work, spiritual despair, and anger at God that separates us from our souls— these are problems that can cause true and profound disruption to our lives. And deep pain. To cope with them, to become stronger during and after them, we need more than what wacky advertisements and sales pitches have to offer. We need capable bodies that help us weather a tough time, and we need the necessary knowledge to use tangible tools at hand when a crisis strikes (insurance procedures, for example, or first aid).

We also need to be aware of how we react emotionally in different crisis situations and how we can allow ourselves to feel deeply without slipping into despair or deep anger and resentment. This is the emotional resilience that many medical professionals speak of when addressing a person's ability to weather a crisis and come through without life-hampering trauma.

Resilience does not mean someone hasn't felt great pain during a crisis, or even afterward. It does mean that the person affected has been able to work through that pain and is putting together a positive life, with manageable or, at least, minimal residual personal and emotional pain.

Along with and throughout our physical and emotional experience during a crisis, we also need spiritual resilience that helps us stand firm as the crisis unfolds.

Spiritual resilience is similar to emotional resilience, with a significant difference: Spiritual resilience allows the person in a crisis the ability to feel supported throughout by not only his or her own resources, but also resources beyond human capabilities. It allows someone to say, "I will get through this time, even if I don't know what all is going to happen, nor how dark the days will get."

Spiritual resilience is the deep, profound support beneath even the most storm-tossed individual. And when nurtured and strengthened, it provides a shield against emotional deterioration and personal despair.

Spiritual Preparedness

Unfortunately, we are so busy in our daily lives that we often neglect to assemble a strong arsenal of spiritual coping tools. What's more, this aspect of managing a crisis isn't foremost in the minds of those we encounter during challenging times—and it's seldom, if ever, part of their response to our crises.

Our doctor might give us a diagnosis and outline a course of treatment, but he or she probably will not assess or make suggestions for our spiritual health.

A first responder arriving on scene of a three-alarm fire is not likely to tell us to evacuate a building and head for a place of quiet where we can calm our nerves.

I have yet to hear a meteorologist who has just predicted a potentially life-threatening storm say, "But, there's hope!"

I have heard more than one psychologist say, "I handle the emotional part (of treating a patient), but I don't talk about anything spiritual."

Each of these professional responses makes sense in one way: spirituality is extremely personal, and even the word *spirituality* means something different for each individual, so it can become an impossible challenge to address it and other perhaps life-threatening issues in a clinical setting.

Also, in today's world, there is probably an overlay of secular political correctness involved; to mention anything spiritual might offend someone. In fact, as the world around us becomes more antiseptic when it comes to spirituality and religion, the importance of spirituality is being rapidly lost in the overall, secular conversation.

Yet, we are more than hollow beings devoid of depth or spiritual presence. Anyone who has loved, laughed, or achieved something positive deep within themselves has experienced this and sensed the soul within, gifted with talents that make up a great reservoir of tools with which we can more than cope with each day, no matter how light or dark, and from which the Spirit works. By strengthening our relationship to that Spirit, we give support to that soul and are better able to act as the courageous people that we inherently are.

So although we might know all about how a backup generator works, or how to use a tire jack in case we get a flat tire while we're out driving, we might not be sure how to shore up our spiritual reservoir, widen and deepen it, or even call upon that inner core when we most need to. Although we attend church, we might not fully appreciate the need and value of daily quiet, meditation, spontaneous (unscripted) prayer, and other personal, spiritual practices to keep us growing and to keep us ready for anything life throws at us.

Although we might understand we have a spiritual as well as a physical and emotional life, we might not be fully aware of what our spiritual skills are, nor what we need to add to our spiritual arsenal to be even more resilient.

Sometimes, spirituality is so distant or something too supernatural to understand that it doesn't seem as if it could be of use in daily life, let alone a crisis. If you have ever heard about someone else's crisis and said, "I don't think I could cope with that if it happened to me," then you understand what I mean. Fortunately, our Spirit is not some distant being in the sky—it's within us to stay. That still, persistent voice within us—God's Spirit—is ever-ready to answer our questions, bring us wisdom, and give us strength. With inspiration, a bit of time, and a lot of faith, we can repel what might otherwise wear us down and fill ourselves with so much strength, determination and resilience that the shadows under the bed or around the corner will be positively glowing with good light!

The Spirit in a Crisis

If our physical and emotional reactions help anchor us, help us understand what we're physically capable of, and give us the ability to express our emotions and move through the full cycle of a crisis, then the Spirit within each of us is the fuel and the fire that enables us to face that pain, that trouble. It gives us discipline to rise each morning and face grim circumstances. It works from within, but it has immense influence over what we do, say, and allow ourselves to feel.

If the body is our physical support structure, and our emotions are the gauge of how deeply we feel loss, pain, and comfort, then the Spirit is the glue that holds us together and allows us to be secure, even in the most precarious of times. It comes from the deepest part of ourselves, and it fuels the faith we need to muster more strength, courage, and creativity in crisis than we ever thought we were capable of.

So many modern-day stories bear this out. For example, selfless medical professionals and even lay people endured great hardship and put themselves in harm's way to render aid to people affected by the Ebola virus in Liberia in 2014 and 2015. Experienced mountaineers and even casual tourists did not hesitate to brave devastated roads, towns, and mountain passes to get to those who were victims of the latest catastrophic earthquake in Nepal.

Closer to home, parents, physicians, first responders, friends, strangers, and other ordinary citizens perform extraordinary feats of selfless bravery and sacrifice. People diagnosed with catastrophic illness exhibit unmatched bravery and compassion as they undergo treatment and act as mentors or role models for patients not as far along in their illness journey. If any one of these heroes had rationally thought of what they were about to do and acted on the mere facts, some if not all would have probably never stepped forward. Why, after all, risk personal safety, health, or comfort when the odds of contracting Ebola, or being injured in one of the many aftershocks stemming from the earthquake in Nepal? Why rush into a burning building if it is probably going to collapse? Why, if the illness is supposed to be terminal, should the patient forge ahead in a clinical trial that might hold the key for others inflicted in the future?

Likewise, if these saints (truly they are saints) had thought of the consequences of seeing so much suffering and pain and only considered this, they might not have decided to render aid. Post-traumatic stress disorder is a real hazard of anyone entering into or already in a place where disaster has struck. Even journalists covering tragedies are at risk of this. But even knowing the terrible odds, the likelihood of negative impact on their own emotional health, these men and women, and others throughout history, still decided to act. Why?

The desire to help and the quality of compassion overpowered any rational reason to retreat. These qualities are not confined to people living in one geographic area or only connected with one ethnic group, race, or religious practice. These traits flow from the Spirit, which we all possess. The more we recognize these traits within us, invite them forward, and use them, the stronger we will be, and the more positive changes we will be able to make before, during, and after a crisis—for ourselves and others.

Of course, we have to dig through a lot of noise to get there. But once the Spirit is engaged and working, great things can happen!

• FOCUS ON FAITH •

Scan stories of disasters for the personal testimonies of survival. Focus on these and not the more negative aspects of the events. Note the amazing courage and ingenuity individuals displayed. Write down one of these stories that stands out in your mind as extraordinary. Find your common ground with this heroic individual and bolster your faith in yourself, the part of you that "could" instead of "can't."

_____

_____

_____

_____

_____

_____

CHAPTER TWO

A Deep Breath

"Start by doing the necessary, then the possible, and suddenly, you are
doing the impossible."
—attributed to St. Francis of Assisi

When a crisis erupts, our first impulse might be to act, but we might
not know how, when, or with what.

The template offered by St. Francis of Assisi gives us a powerful start
to addressing our own crises—beginning with the necessary. I especially connect with Francis's words; as a Midwesterner, practicality is
almost part of my DNA, and considering the necessary first is certainly
practical!

And what could be more necessary than breathing?

Readily available, vital to our survival, and free of charge, physical
breathing is more than inhaling and exhaling, an activity that we often
take for granted. Our breath can signal important health information
and provide us with extra strength and clarity of thought—if we pay
attention to it, cultivate it, and practice it. It plays a role in stress reduction and relief, stamina, physical well-being, and a host of other vital
aspects of living. When looked at in the broader context of how we
spend our time and develop our inner strengths and Spirit, it is something we don't spend enough time mastering.

Breathing can be thought of in several ways, and all of these are
important to well-being. Physically, it is vital; we can go a certain time

without food or water, but we cannot live more than mere minutes without breathing.

Emotionally, breathing affords us personal space to take stock of situations and to help us sort through issues in order to make good decisions. It helps us cultivate good people in our lives and identify and avoid those who might do us harm of any kind.

Spiritually, breathing is that space and time that we give to our conversation with God, to the quiet around and within us that breathes courage, insight, compassion, and truth into the deepest parts of our souls. Through spiritual breathing, we better understand our place in the world, and our purpose, and we can develop wisdom to know how to inspire and help others. Breathing, then, within the context of spiritual resilience, is not only "the necessary" that St. Francis talks about, but it also helps us find what's necessary—to do, think, feel, and become.

Air and Life

When we breathe in oxygen and exhale carbon dioxide and nitric oxide, we are enabling an intricate process of balancing these gases, which our muscles and other parts of our bodies need to function. Too much breathing or not enough upsets the process and causes problems ranging from high blood pressure to anxiety, heightened stress, and possibly, stroke. Those who are breathing impaired have a special appreciation for this delicate balance.

Beneficial or deep breathing can help quell feelings of anxiety and stress, maintain our focus, and enable us to meet physical and emotional challenges, much like an athlete does when competing.

Regular breathing is an activity of the autonomic nervous system, much like when our hearts beat or our eyes blink. We don't think about it. We just do it.

But sometimes, our breath is impacted by external or internal stress or other trauma (or even good news). As with other parts of the body, the breathing process is very sensitive to its place in the body-mind-emotion linkage. It can change in its own unique way when faced with a crisis, and this change, impacting the rate or volume of air in and out, can precipitate responses in other areas of the body, too.

For example, you may know a loved one is going to die and realize you're holding your breath more, waiting for that phone call. This makes you tense and, perhaps, start to feel pain in the stressed parts of your body.

Or work may be piling up at the office and you need to concentrate even harder. You spend hours at work, and you breathe less and less regularly as the hours drag on. Your thoughts become fuzzier, and fatigue washes over you; instead of being more productive with your long efforts, you fear you're producing less!

Or you are about to go into the doctor's office to get lab results and you're feeling afraid; your breath is shallow, and your body is edgy. You clench your jaw. Your fingers tremble.

Breath changes can accompany happy circumstances, too.

Your boyfriend finally proposes, and your breath catches in your throat, or your toddler takes his first steps—and you breathe deeply, in awe of the milestone.

Breath can be an expression of playfulness and humor, as with blowing on a dandelion to scatter it in the wind.

In recent years, researchers have found that breathing has significant effects on our health. Specific breathing disorders, such as sleep apnea, a condition that occurs when we involuntarily stop breathing for brief periods of time in our sleep, is getting a lot of attention because of the potential health risks associated with it, including high blood pressure, diabetes, depression and stroke. Another recently identified syndrome, e-mail or screen apnea, where we stop breathing temporarily while looking at a computer or other screen, may also have negative, long-term effects, as well as a short-term impact on our focus, quality of work, and mood. Someone who is having trouble sleeping or difficulty breathing should work with his or her physician to find the cause and appropriate course of treatment.

HEALTH-FULL BREATHING

Ordinarily, we are unaware of our breath. But sometimes, we might want to use it to reduce stress or as a part of a meditative or exercise practice. One way of breathing that can be useful when we are anxious or feel ourselves become stressed (that fight or flight feeling) is diaphragmatic breathing.[4]

How to do it: Sit quietly and inhale through the nose, feeling your abdomen expand as the air moves deep into your lungs. Then exhale through the mouth easily and slowly. Repeat this a few times as you gauge how well you're responding. At first, some people might become lightheaded, so be particularly vigilant. If this happens, pause the exercise until the lightheadedness has resolved. If this persists, call your doctor.

Diaphragmatic breathing is used by many people, including athletes, musicians (especially singers and wind instrument players), to prepare them for their work. Your doctor can easily show you the proper way to do it, or you can learn from a music teacher or choir director or sports coach. There are Internet resources, too; a very helpful video, provided by the University of Texas Counseling and Mental Health Center gives a brief lesson in diaphragmatic breathing. It is useful to learn and practice it before a crisis or difficult situation arises and you want to call upon it to calm your anxiety. Knowing how to ease feelings of stress using breath can be very empowering, making you more prepared and confident—and less likely to panic!

Other ongoing health-related research is looking at the positive effects of consciously working with our breath to bring down stress levels, quiet the mind, corral those runaway, frazzled nerves, and help us feel better physically, emotionally and spiritually. This research includes Western disciplines such as exercise protocols, as well as physical/spiritual practices such as yoga, Tai Chi, meditation, and massage therapy. Study participants have come from many diverse patient populations, including those suffering from lower back pain or early onset Alzheimer's disease. Some results indicate that this area holds promise for people who want to do something to strengthen their bodies and minds, increase resilience, and build a deeper awareness of how their bodies, minds, and spirits interact and work together. It will be very exciting to see what the future holds for these studies, and those to come!

Breath and the Mind(ful)-Body Connection

Why are many medical professionals becoming more interested in mind-body medicine and alternative or complementary practices and disciplines?

Some of the new research has grown out of real-life experience. Medical school programs include components on spirituality and addressing this and other once-thought non-traditional subjects. Some physicians might also be practitioners of a religion or alternative discipline, and so naturally they are familiar and more fluent in how these relate to the practice of medicine.

Other physicians have had personal experiences with health crises and made discoveries that have led to research and further exploration. One of these is a medical doctor who carved out an intriguing niche in breath therapy and its application to real-life circumstances. For three excruciating years, while establishing his medical career in Germany, Wolf E. Mehling, MD, now associate professor of clinical family and community medicine at the Osher Center for Integrative Medicine, University of California, San Francisco, suffered from chronic lower back pain. During that time, he consulted more than one physician, but no solution was satisfactory.

Of all the chronic health conditions, chronic pain is one that can severely and significantly impact our physical and emotional lives. Chronic pain can add up in terrible ways, making even the youngest person feel depressed, devastated, even disabled. It can take a tremendous toll on relationships, especially because chronic pain is not visible, and the sufferer can often be misunderstood as being lazy or complaining. Chronic pain also has a way of compounding pain on pain, stress on stress. One excruciating limb's pain can soon take over a whole body and a whole life—a crisis-turned-horrific trauma.

When we have chronic pain, we want to do all we can to get rid of it. Of course, we should always consult with our physicians before moving ahead with any kind of therapy or treatment, but we might try to jump from one thing to another, or one supposed sure cure to another, and possibly do ourselves more harm than good. Then, we feel as if we're at a crossroads with no good choices left. If you, like me, have sat on the bed and wept as pain swept over you wave upon wave, you know exactly what I mean.

At twenty-seven or twenty-eight years old, Dr. Mehling did not want to spend the rest of his life crippled by pain. "I did everything under the moon that was possible to do," he told me. "I tried acupuncture, massage, medication."

Dr. Mehling's physicians finally told him that the only option was surgery. But he did not want to do that. "I felt I was too young in my view," he said.

So, he took a step back—a deep breath, literally and figuratively—to find something that would work for him. The answer for him turned out to be breath therapy.

"I attribute my back pain resolving to breath work," Dr. Mehling told me. "It's an old thing, from the 1920s and thirties in Germany. I learned it from an opera singing teacher in Berlin. It's a kind of meditative technique, with the ultimate goal of allowing you to be fully present to the breathing without controlling it."

Dr. Mehling's personal success set him on a novel path to practice medicine and conduct research projects in the United States. One published study, "Randomized, controlled trial of breath therapy for patients with chronic low-back pain,"[5] compared the outcomes of patients who received physical therapy and those who received breath therapy for their chronic lower back pain.

"Patients suffering from chronic lower back pain improved significantly with breath therapy," the study concluded.

Besides pain relief, Dr. Mehling is particularly interested in ways that breath therapy, and other practices that employ conscious breathing techniques or address issues related to the breath, can increase our body awareness and thus help us know what to do to feel healthier, cope better with stress, and become more resilient.

"My personal thinking," Dr. Mehling told me, "is that I believe that people in this stage of civilization have gone more out of their true reality and into computer screens—a virtual reality—and they don't pay attention to their bodies."

This lack of attention can lead to problems if the body is not getting adequate care. But even then, our amazing physical selves do not allow the neglect to continue without calling out for help. This SOS I remember one of my doctors telling me, is akin to our bodies telling us that something is not quite right. We might experience more pronounced pain, sadness, fatigue, or other cues to do something beneficial to rebalance and heal. And when we do, we are rewarded with a better sense of well-being.

Dr. Mehling feels our bodies often call for us to do beneficial things, for example, go to the gym or have more quiet time, in order to function well and cope with life. "Think of it," he said, "you get a massage, you go to the gym, and you feel so much better. Your personal awareness of the body, that's what's missing."

And, let us not forget, too, the personal awareness of the Spirit.

I think that the Spirit does much the same thing as our body does when we are neglectful of our inner, soul-filled life. As we fail to make time for solitude and true quiet, as we feed ourselves a constant diet of bad news, conflict, and worry, and as we strive to do things that rub against the unique goodness and creativity that we possess inside, we feel depressed, anxious, and definitely off-balance. Yet, when we take the time to listen to the cues the Spirit feeds us, and when we spend focused time allowing quiet, inviting the Spirit to cleanse our minds and hearts during a roiled time in our lives, we feel better having done it, and we are better and stronger for it.

To develop physical, emotional, and spiritual awareness takes time and focused attention. But once we begin and the benefits multiply, we realize how wonderful and important our investment of time and focus is!

Where to Begin?
I was never fond of exercise. Having been very ill as a child (thirteen pneumonias before I was eighteen years old, among other illnesses), I missed the life lesson on hand-eye coordination. Oh, I tried various

sports (I couldn't skip gym class every day). But I was more inclined to duck and cover than dash and catch!

What I did do, even if I was feeling ill, was play my clarinet and sing. From an early age, I loved music and it was not unusual for me to spend three hours after school holed up in my room practicing my clarinet. It was also not unusual for me to join as many choral groups as would let me in!

• FAITH IN FOCUS •

Think of a specific time when you had to learn a new skill. For example, deftly dribbling a basketball, preparing a delicious omelet, or giving a public talk. Maybe, that first time, you lost the ball, dropped the eggs, or were so nervous that your voice cracked. Think about your learning process and how much better you are now than then. Have faith that each time you consciously devote attention and quiet to spiritual breathing you will get better!

_____

_____

_____

_____

_____

_____

Little did I realize that I was learning valuable lessons on diaphragmatic breathing, breath control, self-discipline, and the health-promotion aspects of making music (more on this later). The benefits of regular practice played out (please pardon the pun—it's one of my shortcomings, but I am working on it) in tremendous enjoyment and a good sense of accomplishment. My musical youth also helped hone patience; with enough practice, I believed I would eventually make my way through complicated musical phrases and polish those rough spots in tone and technique. So it was easier to devote long hours to practice because it was not a sacrifice, but rather a process toward a very desirable goal.

Today, I hold onto the beneficial aspect of discipline, as well as the sense of a learning curve whenever I set out to learn or accomplish anything (or practice anything, such as regular, deep breathing)—or even write a book. As with a crisis, there is a beginning, middle, and end. The only way to get to a good end is to devote good time to each part of the process that leads to it!

But how, specifically, can someone get to that good end, benefiting from body and spiritual awareness so that he or she can strengthen and become more resilient?

Faith traditions have wonderful resources, including some like Catholicism, that are centuries old, from which you can learn about prayer, meditation, and other contemplative practices. Just as breathing is readily available, these, too, might be right next door to you (or right at home), especially if you are already active within a church or other faith community.

Many other activities can cultivate a better sense of breathing and body awareness in our lives. Yoga, meditation, Tai Chi, and combinations or blends of these provide formal avenues for body awareness-building and platforms for self-discovery. Stress relief classes offered by local health centers or hospitals can also be helpful, especially if they address any underlying medical conditions that might also be a factor in your overall health. Some examples of these are diabetes support groups or smoking cessation clinics.

If you're new to the world of alternative practices, it might be helpful to sit in on a class first. Your doctor might have good advice tailored to your specific physical capabilities, other health considerations, and the resources available. Your parish priest or clergyperson might also be able to give you a referral.

Another option is to learn a sport or get a different approach to one you already play. A good coach will know how breathing impacts how you play, and with this information, you can develop awareness of your breath—on and off the court or field.

Sometimes, a combination of practices can be helpful, especially if other areas of life are in constant flux; it might not be possible to commit to a weekly yoga class, for example, but a periodic class combined with daily time spent in prayer and meditation can make a powerful inner-strengthening routine. Even videos or websites can be valuable tools.

But, how do we, individually, find the time and place to get into the routine of quiet, self-examination, and that important courage- and strength-building that we need to meet the great challenges of living?

Most of us cannot just quit our jobs or leave our families and go to a pristine mountaintop to spend our days meditating. Moreover, for many of us, just thinking of quiet gets drowned out by life's many noises—external bells and whistles and internal doubt and anxiety. How do we overcome all of this to benefit from deep breathing? How in the world can we hack away at all the over- and undergrowth in our lives to find the right path?

Then, there are practical things. How do we pay for the classes and gear? How do we schedule time with traffic, family responsibilities, and work pressure to dig in and succeed?

Did you notice as you read the last few paragraphs that you might have slowed or stopped breathing?

Take a deep breath—now.

Exhale slowly.

Now, take another breath. Exhale slowly.

Close your eyes for a moment and listen to your regular breath. Give it time to calm.

Just breathe. And when you feel a bit more relaxed, continue reading.

This exercise, a modified meditative breathing activity, probably took you less than two minutes, start to finish. It didn't require special clothing, environment, or financial outlay. It wasn't included on a highly produced DVD or MP3 file.

Yet, think about the benefit you received from it. Maybe you felt a little more relaxed? Maybe you simply appreciated the break in reading?

Now, think about multiplying that benefit by many times when you develop a regular habit or practice of stopping, breathing, and looking within. What kind of difference to your overall life would that relaxation, understanding, and calm make? Why not begin to find out?

• FAITH IN FOCUS •

Write down all of your activities during the day, from preparing a meal to work, to evening routines. Put a check mark by the things that are absolutely necessary for you to do. Now, look at the list and, of the items not checked, select three that you could cross off and, in their place, put time for breathing and other stress-relieving activities. Have faith that you can and will keep that time for days to come.

Of course, there are many other things that we consider necessary in our lives. We have responsibilities, others depend upon us, and we live in a work- and results-driven world. But our basic life and health, and our inner Spirit are important, too. Body awareness gives us better understanding about how we react to a variety of life events crisis hits. It helps us know when to "fight" and when to step back, regroup, and rest. It helps us in how we relate to others. Whether you start to culti-vate a deeper sense of your body and how it works and moves and reacts through prayer, yoga, Tai Chi, meditation, by just sitting quietly, or some other practice, deep breathing figures prominently in quieting the distractions and allowing us to listen and begin to discern what we are meant to do.

• FAITH IN FOCUS •

A good way to get some experience in building body awareness is to practice mindful moments. Pause at various points during the day and be aware of when you hold your breath, or when your breath is irregular. Turn your thoughts inward and focus for a moment on what cues your body and Spirit might be sending you. Note them, and promise your-self that you will work on resolving them. Have faith that, with time and patience, you can relax and rebalance, allowing yourself to enjoy greater internal strength and confidence.

_____

_____

_____

_____

_____

The same basic principles of physical deep breathing that help us become more aware, calm, and strong can be applied specifically and practically to emotional and spiritual needs, too. I call these areas "emotional deep breathing" and "spiritual deep breathing" because in both, we take profound time and attention to understand and address critical flash points or stressors that affect us in negative and sometimes unhealthful ways. As with physically taking deep breaths, the more we practice techniques to allow ourselves breathing room of an emotional or spiritual nature, the more ready we will be to use these as tools during a crisis.

Emotional Deep Breathing

Our emotions set us apart from all other creatures made by God, and they are wonderful conduits for human expression and understanding. But sometimes, crises can disrupt our hearts so much that these very emotions become more of a burden than a blessing, and we might not know exactly how to express them and, thus, benefit from them and bring this benefit to the situation at hand.

For example, some people might be afraid to express sorrow, anger, frustration, or deep grief in front of others, and they might even feel guilty expressing these very human emotions in private, too. One parent I spoke with felt she had to lock herself in her bathroom and run the water loudly before she could cry over the tragic death of a grandchild. Another man, head of his household, brought extra tremendous stress upon himself because he could not acknowledge painful fear and frustration of being on the edge of financial ruin.

In these and other similar situations, emotions that are bottled up inside have a way of coming out sooner or later, often in ways that we do not mean. Anger might be expressed in lashing out at a stranger in a store, for example, or we might turn on someone we trust and in so doing drive a bitter wedge between ourselves and the person who might otherwise be supportive. In such cases, emotional deep breathing can give us time and invite wisdom to diffuse highly charged situations—and provide a venue for expression of that which seems, to us, inexpressible.

When I think of a biblical example of emotional deep breathing, I think of Jesus hearing about the death of his very good friend, Lazarus. Jesus, a spiritual leader and strong man, did not try to hide his grief from others. In John's Gospel, "Jesus wept," and he was not deterred even by the barbs from some onlookers, who criticized him for not working a miracle so Lazarus would not have died. Nor was he side-tracked by expressing his grief. After weeping, Jesus then continued with his ministry, ultimately raising Lazarus from the dead.

There is a beautiful symbolism in the tears that wash from our eyes and the water that washes our souls in baptism, as well as the physical water that cleanses our bodies. And beyond poetry, crying is one of the physical ways we can emotionally cleanse ourselves, releasing sorrow and spending pent-up grief and then moving ahead with clear eyes and a clearer heart.

Laughter, too, is a way of releasing emotions that might destabilize us, especially in dire situations. Finding a way to laugh can unfreeze tension within ourselves and relax us so that we can better accept a tough situation and do what we need to cope with it. I have found laughter to be one of my most powerful emotional deep breathing tools, especially when dealing with the life-altering effects of lupus.

During one particularly frightening episode, I was having great difficulty swallowing solid food and liquids. Tests revealed that I had three separate problems with my esophagus and that, together, they created a perfect storm for choking. I was assigned to a swallow therapist who worked with me about how I might eat and drink more safely. As we finished one session, she said, "Now, I do recommend that whenever you eat out you have someone with you who knows the Heimlich maneuver."

I felt a chill come over me as those words sank in, flooding over any bit of denial I might have. At that point, I could have broken down right there in the stark hospital hallway. But a very different emotion surfaced, one that I had cultivated for years: humor.

I began to laugh.

The therapist looked panicked. "What's wrong? Are you all right?"

"Oh, I'm fine," I replied, taking a moment to take a deep (physical) breath. "I'm just thinking that this will make for an interesting conversation if someone asks me out on a date. "Yes, I'll go out with you, but do you know the Heimlich maneuver?"

I walked away, looking back to see the therapist still staring at me, shaking her head.

Far from being wrong, my response to the esophageal realities was exactly right and allowed me to build courage and determination for difficult days (and conversations) ahead. And I continue to build on my sense of humor by trying each day to find something to laugh about in a positive, uplifting, Spirit-supporting way.

Another powerful emotion that grows ever-brighter with careful cultivation is love. All the positive steps we take to help ourselves be healthy and strong are expressions of the love we have for the precious lives we are given—loving, emotional deep breaths that grow light within us and make us stronger throughout life's ups and downs. As we love others, too, we create an uplifting, stress-fighting environment for ourselves and our loved ones. When we love, we accept ourselves and others, and we create a safe harbor for deep expressions of other emotions during the times that try us or elate us. We foster security through love, and when we are feeling most weak, our ability to breathe deeply, emotionally, fills us up with hope.

We can exercise this kind of loving by consciously surrounding ourselves with what is good, strong, and true, and by encouraging positive relationships that inspire all that is good within us.

• FAITH IN FOCUS •

What makes you laugh? Cry? Cower? What makes you angry? What tugs at your heart with unmistakable love? Are you afraid to express any of your emotions? As you build greater awareness of your body's responses to crises and other situations, notice your emotions, their force, and the way you do or do not express them. Have faith that as you better understand and cope with your emotions, you will be able to respond more confidently and positively.

_____

_____

_____

_____

_____

_____

Sometimes, situations stir up tremendous anger in our hearts. Injustices, random acts of violence, and other events can be terribly hurtful, and we can be so thrown off balance by them that we might want to respond with hurt, inflicting pain where we have been pained. But as we see throughout history, current events, and even in our own personal relationships, injuring others because of the injury to ourselves only creates more violence.

It is important to understand that the emotion of anger is quite natural, especially when the pain is personal. It is also important to separate this human emotion from actions that might ensue that are not positive at all, including violence, obsession with the negative event, or unwillingness to let go of pain. Seeking professional help from a counselor, clergyperson, or physician can be a valuable way to help us gain perspective and control of anger or other emotions that are out of balance. This can also help us develop appropriate ways to express our emotions.

Through this supportive and guided emotional deep breathing, we can understand our more turbulent feelings, including anger, in a safe environment, and accept and cope with them without letting them foster potentially damaging actions that hurt us and others.

Our emotions might develop or grow over time, but in their purest form, they have a shining, childlike quality. Weeping, laughing, sighing, getting angry, or feeling anxious—these benefit from time spent understanding and appreciating them as the gifts that they are, gifts with which we express our feelings and breathe deeply from an amazing well of emotion both blessed and blessedly human.

Spiritual Deep Breathing
Spiritual deep breathing fills our souls with wisdom, compassion, and clarity, and provides a constant underpinning of trust and truth that we are not facing life's crises alone, and that we need not fear being overwhelmed by sudden upheavals. Spiritual deep breathing allows us the time and space to find more courage, purpose, and direction so that we avoid doing what might be less beneficial and embrace what is most helpful. It can be a way to dive deep into past hurts and resolve them, so that these do not fester and become impediments to resolving crises that have yet to occur. And it can be an excellent way to learn about and

appreciate the precious person, the beautiful life that you are, without the glare of others' judgment or society's prism to get in the way.

Like physically taking a deep breath, spiritual deep breathing need not be a complicated process, nor does it require anything as elaborate as traveling to a high mountaintop to find the meaning of life. It does not even hinge upon going to church every week or joining one or another religious groups.

No, spiritual deep breathing can take place very close to home—at home, in fact—and thus, it can be a powerful support before, during, and after a shattering life event. In fact, when you establish a supportive, quiet place close-by and go to it regularly, it becomes like the Edenic retreat many of us envision as the perfect place to go, rejuvenate, reflect, and gather strength for the challenges ahead.

In our spiritual breathing place, we can hear God.

Spiritual Breathing in Action

For thirteen years, I conducted an African American, Catholic gospel choir at a church near south Los Angeles. I have many wonderful memories from that time, but within the context of facing crises and emotional-spiritual breathing, one really stands out.

Marilyn White, a soprano in the choir, arrived at church a little late one Sunday morning. As she zipped up her choir robe and joined us in the prayer circle, she raised her voice to pray for her son. The night before, he'd been the victim of a drive-by shooting on a street not far from his college dorm in Atlanta. He was in the hospital, and his condition was serious, his prognosis unclear.

Of course, everyone in the choir surrounded her (and her son) with love, support, and especially prayer. As I joined hands with the group and bowed my head, my heart broke for this dear mother and for her son, who had such a bright future ahead of him. But I was stunned, too, that she had come to church that morning as usual instead of getting on the first plane out to Atlanta.

Little did I realize that I was about to learn a huge lesson in the importance of taking a deep and deeply spiritual breath.

After we prayed, I asked my friend why she'd decided to postpone her trip so she could come to Mass. With a smile, she replied, "The devil would have wanted me to skip church, but I'm not going to let him have that. I have to be here, to sing, pray, and praise God. Then, I'll go."

Years later, when we talked about that difficult period, she explained further why she had to come to church before traveling to her son's hospital bed.

"It wasn't a knee-jerk time," Marilyn said. "It was a knee-bending time. I knew my son was in God's hands, and I knew what I had to do before I went to be with him."

How extraordinary that was and is! I am not a mother, but I think in this situation, my first reaction would have been to jump on the first plane out to be with my son. Certainly, many of us have experienced other situations where our first impulse is to spring into action. Get out of our vehicle that has just been rear-ended and yell at the offending driver. Jump to the worst case scenario of a scary medical diagnosis. Elbow our way through those tending to the situation and insist we take control instead—the fight response.

Or the opposite might be true; we might think we are in such bad shape that we retreat (the flight response), and we simply cannot muster any courage to face the things we so desperately need to do. There could be a physical reason for this. Perhaps, when that fateful telephone call comes, our heart rate spikes and we're propelled into action by the sudden adrenaline coursing through us. Or we're so struck with nerves that we simply cannot sit still. Or we are so stunned by what's happening that our brains and our hearts simply cannot take it all in and make sense of it.

Yes, if we act before thinking, or we don't think at all, we allow the event to take over ourselves, and we might not do what actually needs to be done, the "necessary," as mentioned by St. Francis of Assisi.

This is where breathing comes in. Physical breath, of course, deep, diaphragmatic breaths to calm us and remind us of our profound center. Emotional breath that gives expression to our feelings. And vital spiritual breath.

Crucial time spent taking a soul-reaching, time-with-God breath can make the difference between messing up an already messed-up situation (and ourselves) or having the inner strength, the core of confidence, to know and do what will make the most good out of bad. It can invigorate trust that there is a reason for the pain and loss, even if the outcome is unclear, and the journey through crisis has just begun. A spiritual deep breath is exactly what Marilyn took on the day after she received news about her son.

She was concerned, of course. What loving mother would not be? Her only, precious son was lying in a far-off hospital, the victim of senseless violence. But her strong faith, which she had nurtured for decades, had allowed her to do more than be concerned. It had given her clarity of mind and heart. She trusted that her son was in good medical hands, and that God was watching over him and his medical team. She benefited from the in-person dose of love and support from her home church community before making the long, solitary journey across the country. Only with a steadfast spirit, exercised in prayer and action, could she face the uncertain days ahead and give her son the support he needed to recover.

So it was not a knee-jerk but a knee-bending response, which was very natural and familiar to her, that allowed her to stand firm when she most needed to.

Physically, Marilyn's deep breath had benefit, too; choral singing is a fun, beautiful, and athletic activity that involves deep, diaphragmatic breathing. Singing with a choir has been shown through some research to be an excellent way to de-stress the body, develop internal focus and discipline, and strengthen the heart. Another intersection of mind-heart-body-and-soul medicine!

I've learned other lessons of spiritual and emotional deep breathing, some from people whose lives were not only full of crises and busyness, but personal danger and, sometimes, doubt. Many others who have faced crises have also discovered the importance of the deep breath, the personal moment, before acting on the particular challenge facing them. Each one was different, of course, but they have some strong themes tying them together through years, distance, and cultures.

Moses went to the mountaintop, prayed and listened to God, and descended with God's Word and a purpose.

Gandhi developed a firm and unwavering practice of meditation, which allowed him to take abundant deep breaths in the face of tremendous obstacles and crises.

Noah, whose story we will get to in the next chapter, prayed—and listened—to God as the plan to flood the world unfolded. He had a very busy life, full of family and work responsibilities. But even in his everyday existence, he clearly took time to be quiet enough to discern how God was moving in the world and what that meant for his life.

St. Francis of Assisi's life is full of amazing accomplishments, not the least of which was the establishment of a far-reaching religious order of brothers that transformed the Catholic Church and the world. But in order to achieve these long-lasting changes—and to withstand the many crises that arose from his life's work—he sought quiet and stark simplicity in a cave in what is now called the Eremo delle Carceri, near Assisi. There, his spiritual and emotional deep breathing consisted of prayer, meditation, and dreaming, through which he sought wisdom and strength.

Jesus went to the desert or other retreats regularly, even when large crowds were clamoring for his help and presence. In the three, short years of his ministry, we might expect he'd double-book his calendar so he could fit in as much of his Father's work as possible, but instead, he showed by his example that quiet in prayer and reflection is as much a part of an active life of service as the actions themselves.

Today, perhaps you go to the riverbank, into a dense forest, or even a corner of your room. Maybe your breathing place changes periodically due to a move or other necessity. Or you find that your body needs someplace different as you age.

The importance of your breathing place is not so much that it is large or small, cramped or spacious, or even constant. The important thing is that you are in an environment where you can hear yourself pray, think, and breathe. Although it might seem as if you are taking a retreat from others, spiritual deep breathing on a regular basis is essential to keep your inner calm, wisdom, and emotional health. Far from being cowardly or selfish, it is through these sessions of silence and solitude that you can become stronger and more giving. But to benefit fully from this practice, you have to commit to a regular and steady routine.

FAITH IN FOCUS

Consider all of the places you can go to when you have to breathe deeply. Which one is most convenient and helpful to you when you need to get away? Write a description of this place and note why it is so special for you. Take a picture of it and tuck it into your journal. Revisit it frequently, in mind or physically, and enjoy the solitude you find there.

Regular Practice

As a young musician whose instruments, voice and clarinet, rely on proper breathing technique, I experienced firsthand the need to practice regularly. This was not only so that I could learn the notes, but so that I could exercise my breathing muscles and build up stamina. Each day, I could feel myself grow a little stronger, more sure, and able to tackle greater and greater challenges with the firm foundation I laid with solid practice. I also realized that, some days, I am not at my best—I'm more or less tired, distracted, sick, or rushed. Even so, the regularity of practice helped me understand that these bad days were not the norm and that I could have faith that my work was not in vain.

The same is true for our ability to use breath throughout daily life, especially in crises. Besides the physical muscles used in breathing, spiritual breathing involves developing a discipline so that it becomes more natural to take time out of busyness and rely on deep, spiritual solitude and quiet to find calm and wisdom. Practicing it on a regular basis also helps to reinforce the knowledge that there is a cycle to building strength, just as there is a cycle to crises; each day will not be exactly the same as all the others, and some days will find us more pulled apart from quiet than others. But if we persist, over time the benefits of spiritual breathing will become so beneficial to us that we will *want* to seek it, to *make* the time to be still.

At first, it is that time element that might seem most elusive, but there are undoubtedly several moments in the day when you could pause and reflect; even small moments add up over time and practice. Or you might learn, as you dissect your calendar, that there is hidden time—partial hours between activities, for example. This regular time each day can also be helpful to begin your practice of seeking solitude and space in which to breathe.

Supports, such as classes in one of many practices that involve deep breathing, including yoga, meditation, or Tai Chi, can be useful to establish formal ways to approach your quiet time. These can also have physical benefits, as mentioned above, and the regularity of going to class can help you establish a more natural sense of how breathing fits in with your life.

Another approach is to learn more about how breathing impacts your exercise, or if you do not exercise or play a sport regularly, you might ask your doctor for suggestions about how you can begin, with breath being a component in the activity that you take up.

Regular prayer and faith-centered reading are other activities that can be enhanced by deep and cleansing breath. For example, instead of praying from a long list of petitions, pause between each person or thing on the list and take two slow, complete breaths—inhaling and exhaling while mindfully offering your prayer to God. Or when you read a passage from the Bible or other sacred book, breathe in and out before you begin and then pause a few times throughout your reading. Breathe, think, reread the passages, and let the words sink into your heart just as the health-bringing air fills and cleanses you.

A getaway or retreat can be a good way to begin a dedicated effort to find more time for spiritual breathing and reflection. It is also helpful for reinforcing spiritual work that you do more regularly. However, sometimes we begin to feel as if we have to get away in order to recoup and rewind our inner selves. We let tension and stress build up as we anticipate getting away, and we ignore the opportunities we have near home, at home, within ourselves to have time each day, even during work or school.

Just as physical breathing is with us, inside of us, and capable of providing us with good benefit, so too is the nearby opportunity for spiritual growth and strengthening—as long as we give ourselves the permission to take it.

Spiritual Breathing, Rest, and Sleep

One of the first things that is usually disrupted when you are in a crisis (or worrying about one) is your ability to sleep. Perhaps your mind is racing, stewing over the current problems and potential ones to come. Practical matters can interfere with sleep patterns—an uncomfortable place to sleep, long days that cut into our regular bedtime and when we arise. Others might undermine your sleep time, too, whether in the same room (a snoring spouse, for example) or across the country (time differences and those oh-so-early or late telephone calls). Medical conditions like sleep apnea can affect the duration and quality of sleep.

But sleep is crucial to health and, especially, your clarity of mind and heart. If you're sleep deprived, you function less well during the day. Problems seem greater. Solutions seem harder to grasp. You might find your emotions heightened, especially anger, frustration, and sorrow. Long-term lack of sleep can adversely affect your physical health, too. Far from being dormant during sleep, your body is engaged in numerous processes of rebuilding, renewing, and fortifying. Physically, you need those hours of sleep in order to allow necessary internal maintenance to run its course so that you can function optimally when you are awake.

New parents, city dwellers, late-shift workers, and others will appreciate that sometimes a good night's sleep is impossible. Yes, things do go bump and "waaah!" in the night. But prolonged, regular disruptions of sleep are not only unhealthful, they are unproductive to doing your very best. And as you become more stressed about not getting sleep, you'll find that you are even less able to sleep. Not a comfortable cycle but a very painful one!

Because there can be medical reasons for an inability to get restorative sleep, it is always a good idea to consult with your physician if you have ongoing problems getting to or staying asleep. Before your appointment, keep a sleep log that shows things such as the activities you did before going to bed, what you ate and when, what time you started to try to sleep, what time you fell asleep (approximately), and how often you woke up during the night. Sleep studies and other research are more readily available today, so it is more possible to address and treat sleep disorders once they are identified.

Besides consulting your physician, here are some other things that I have found helpful to promoting relaxation and sleep:
• Regular, mindful prayer or meditation during the day has relaxing benefits when you're trying to get to sleep at night; keep up a regular practice and let that serve as a basis for before-bedtime relaxing.
• Evening prayer that focuses on God's love, comfort, and protection can help turn off the litany of problems that might run through your mind and stop you from drifting off to sleep.
• A place that is only for sleep signals to the body and mind that no other distractions will interfere with getting a good

night's sleep; bedrooms set up as media centers have a way of adding stress, not relieving it!

• Putting a buffer zone of at least an hour around bedtime is important to preparing your mind and heart for sleep; avoid lengthy, complex conversations, negative topics, arguments, or troubleshooting computer problems. (This I have learned from emotionally painful experience!)

When we understand and appreciate the immense, necessary role that breathing plays in life and in stress reduction, we can be truly grateful that this is a gift readily and abundantly available to us. Deep breath brings healing, time for reflection, and promotes wellness throughout the day and night.

As we find our own, individual ways to bring more breathing benefits to our lives, whether in a formal practice or simply more mindful moments, we build an ever-deeper, internal foundation of strength from which we can navigate even the most complex journeys of life. From that basis of internal calm and awareness, faith grows as fear dissolves.

CHAPTER THREE

What *Is*, Not What *If*

It's no wonder that successful scary movies employ the technique of suspense—not overtly showing the monster, villain, or other disaster-in-the-making, but by lingering on the looming shadow, the hints of doom, the music slowly building to a crack or a scream.

Yes, one of the greatest panic-inducing elements of crises (and even the thought of one) is the fear of the unknown, and its cornerstone is the naggingly unhelpful game of "What if... ?"

"What if the mole on my back is cancer?"

"What if I go into work tomorrow, and the boss fires me?"

"What if my cousin isn't telling me everything about what's in our grandfather's will?"

"What if, once my son begins high school, he starts taking drugs?"

"What if I die before my spouse?"

"What if I mess up during my big speech, and everyone laughs?"

"What if...?" goes all the way back to the Garden of Eden and Adam and Eve (and we know how well that question worked out for them)! But today, the speed of communication paired with the overbooked lives we lead make us not only play the game, we live it.

On the Internet, no sooner do we hear of a disaster anywhere in the world than we see an avalanche of tweets and texts about it and the speculation of similar events coming to our shores, too. Personal news, too, travels lightning-fast, and it also touches many lives besides those of the people immediately involved in it. The world, large and small, is thus highly personalized to us—streaming on a screen readily at hand or at home. All of the troublesome information we digest can have a serious, cumulatively negative impact on our sensitive spirits.

This isn't because we absolutely delight in lapping up negative news (although, if we feed ourselves a steady diet of it, it can become habitual). Much of our exposure to the woes in the world—far away or nearby—is due to the age in which we live.

Think of these two disasters, separated by time and place, but sharing a commonality—utter destruction of people and property.

On August 24, in the year A.D. 79, the thriving city of Pompeii, as well as several other nearby towns, were completely destroyed by the volcanic eruption of Mount Vesuvius. It was an enormous disaster, but news of it took months, even years, to circulate throughout the entire Roman Empire and beyond; it was not until a few years after the event that the Younger Pliny, who witnessed the event firsthand, wrote to a friend about his experience near the epicenter of destruction.

With such information time-lag, most people who heard of the devastation had no reason to worry that their own destruction might be imminent; they'd already lived well beyond what might even remotely be considered reasonable time from the moment Vesuvius exploded. Moreover, for centuries, no one could fully comprehend the full and awful effect of the eruption; Pompeii lay under tons of ash, pumice, and other debris for centuries before excavation finally began in 1748. It was not until the nineteenth century that a more systematic excavation revealed substantial details about the destructive event, and even today, that work is ongoing.

By contrast, on March 11, 2011, a massive earthquake of a magnitude 9.0 struck off the coast of Japan, and almost immediately, Twitter and other social media erupted with firsthand news, including video footage and photos. Seismologists issued warnings and advisories of a possible tsunami in the hours after the initial shockwave, not only in the region of Japan, but also North America. I remember well the red-highlighted advisory scrolling along the bottom of my television screen and the piercing beeps that punctuated its continuous loop, and how my mind cartwheeled to, "OK, stop everything and figure out what we should do in case of a tsunami!" Truly, the disaster had an immediate and profound impact on more than just those near the event.

Pompeiians had no true warning that disaster was imminent; there had been rumblings from Vesuvius for days prior, and earthquakes rattling the city, but these were not thought of as anything but normal. So most of the people in the city tried to evacuate too late, many dying while running through the streets, down stairways, or taking what they thought was shelter at home. Today, we are blessed that technology has developed to the point where we can have some forewarning of many dangers and then take steps to protect ourselves. We're fortunate to live in a time when we understand more about the relation between different climate events, too.

But the contrast between how news of disasters affected people centuries ago and how it can affect us now is important to understand, too. The more frequently we are exposed to bad news, and the more personal and close it seems to us, amplified as it travels to and from us, the more likely we will fold it into our heart's basket of worry. And over time, the more on edge we might feel—and the more likely to panic when a true crisis does occur.

Other, less dangerous, venues contribute to our exposure to worrisome what-ifs, including advertisements, daily speech, and our own thoughts. For example, a coworker's seemingly innocent, "What if we don't get that sale?" can set off a small chain of worry (such questions seldom prompt positive responses, unless we work hard at them). Other nagging doubts in our own minds stir up what-if moments that, if not handled with a deep breath of "I cannot worry about what I cannot control," can truly burrow deep within us.

Our God-given creativity is a wonderful asset, a bright and nimble talent that longs to be put to strong purpose. Fed with doubt and worry, that creativity will go off in many different directions, each leading us to scenarios and conclusions that circle and feed back into our worry-clouded thoughts. But if we corral our creativity to focus on the other side of the what-if, we can really move forward.

For example, asking "What if...?" can become a way of trouble-shooting in order to develop a plan to deal with a potential disaster, such as a fire or other emergency. It can serve as the basis for writing intriguing stories or embarking on significant medical research. The positive what-if can drive innovation, negotiate peace, and reimagine whole communities. Asking, "What if...?" can become a problem solver, instead of a problem maker. A support and not a mental and emotional burden that keeps us awake and anxious at night. But how?

The individuals I've already mentioned had a singularly strong bent toward spiritual and physical deep breathing—the soprano at my church, St. Francis of Assisi, Gandhi, and even Noah. They took time apart from others and the more skeptical elements of their worlds and spent time thinking, praying, meditating, and gathering strong faith. Jesus Christ did this, too; although he was God, he still distanced himself from others at times and prayed.

Then, they figured out what resources they had at hand and began to act.

The second part of the quote from St. Francis of Assisi that headed up chapter 2 says it best: "Start by doing the necessary, then the *possible*, and suddenly, you are doing the impossible" (my emphasis). It's that "possible" that we next need to find, focus on, and embrace. The actual, tangible, real assets we possess and the resources we have at hand to tackle our problems and bring ourselves more calm with which to live through challenging days.

Relying on the possible, first, before jumping to what-ifs and the thought of bad outcomes, gives us an inventory of resources that we can use in any situation. This inventory allows us to see we have many tools, real tools, to work with. These tools give us assurance that we are not helpless in times of crisis. From that position of strength, we are then able to shed the shadows of worry and make a plan to truly handle, beat back, and overcome our challenges. We can give the effort our all because we know what our all is.

There, especially, is the origin of our active strength and courage: Not being victim to the what-if, but rather, understanding and utilizing each *what-is*. To get to this point, we have to know what we have to work with. More importantly, we have to bring inspiration to that use, and a strong spirit to overcome self-doubt, which can be a powerful impediment to successful resilience.

Being Prepared

One of my favorite what-is, not what-if, stories that highlights the crucial role of the Spirit is also one of the oldest stories in the Bible: the story of Noah and the flood. Even if you are not a person of faith, I think you'll find that this story illustrates vividly how an inner life of contemplation and prayer can cut through idle speculation and escalating trouble and allow someone to have great clarity—enough to know what's needed, and how and when to weather a crisis (no pun intended).

Noah had a serious problem. An upstanding man with a family and respected standing in his community, he lived at a time when people around him were engaged in "wickedness" (Genesis 5–9). Some of us can relate to Noah; it is not easy to continue to try to be a good person when everyone around you is doing wrong. At the very least, it is stressful. At the worst, it can be dangerous.

Yes, Noah must have had significant, daily problems. But everyday living was not his biggest problem. Noah's much more serious problem was trouble of a divine nature.

He was a man of faith. We know from Genesis that he prayed to God. This was the God of his forefathers, all the way back through his lineage to Adam. It was the God who had made the earth and all the creatures upon and above it, who made man "in his image" (Genesis 1:27). Noah trusted God, and most importantly, in his time spent in prayer, he listened to what God had to say to him.

After creating the earth and all life there, God "looked at everything he made, and he found it very good" (Genesis 1:31). But soon, that goodness began to turn sour. The earth became more populated, and people engaged in more wickedness, the same bad behavior surrounding upstanding Noah and his family.

God became more and more displeased with his creation because of their decadence. Finally, He was "sorry that [He] had made them" (Genesis 6:7) and decided to destroy everything and everyone except Noah, his family, and two of each of every species of creature on the earth.

Thus began Noah's truly immense problem.

Imagine if you lived as Noah did, surrounded on all sides by wrong-doing, corrupt people. It's a struggle, but you work hard, still, to keep your faith and prayer life solid and provide for your family besides. Then, one day, as you pray, God tells you, "I will destroy the whole world, except for you and your family and two of each of every species of creature"?

After you take a very deep breath, your mind might race headlong with what-ifs. After all, you are praying, not sitting across a table from

God, not physically standing in front of him.

"What if I'm not understanding this correctly?"

"What if I'm going crazy?"

"What if this is only a bad dream?"

Noah had no way to fact-check a conversation with God. However, remember how Noah lived his life, remember how he prayed—God was part of his life, part of his world. Noah had learned through time and effort to hear and listen to God.

Through practice of anything, we develop the ability to hear off notes, to discern when we're not hitting the ball correctly or not speaking clearly. We understand where we go wrong in making the perfect lasagna or driving with standard transmission. We also know when we're on the right track, when our efforts are bearing good fruit.

And so, when we have a steady, solid practice of developing and maintaining a strong awareness of ourselves inside and out, we fine-tune our listening. We become sensitive to the world around us, too. Then, in a constant practice of prayer and other quiet pursuits, we are able to hear God more clearly, specifically, and truly—and know what gifts (tools) we possess.

In Genesis, I believe it is telling that we do not hear that Noah peppered God with questions, such as "How do we survive?" "When is this going to happen?" or "How will it all end?"

Rather, Noah listened carefully to all that God had to say. Not just the dramatic and horrific declaration of destruction, but all the crucial details, the tangible things that Noah had to do to survive.

And, my, yes, God gave Noah details!

Make yourself an ark of cypress wood; make rooms in the ark, and cover it inside and out with pitch. This is how you are to make it: the length of the ark three hundred cubits, its width fifty cubits, and its height thirty cubits. Make a roof for the ark, and finish it to a cubit above; and put the door of the ark in its side; make it with lower, second, and third decks. (Genesis 6:14–16)

God then told Noah how he was going to destroy the earth and what Noah needed to do to load the ark so that his family and the other creatures would be saved. Then, he left Noah to his task. All Noah had to do next was build the ark, herd everyone and everything into it, and ride out the floods—while he continued to survive in daily life!

What if you were instructed to do something as serious and as monumental as Noah, but you still had to put food on the table and take care of your family while you were doing it? Moreover, what if you had to convince the members of your family that God had truly spoken to you, instructed you specifically, and there was no time to waste because your survival depended upon completing everything before the floods engulfed the earth?

Do you think that all of those lawless, corrupt people around you would sit by and merely watch as you started construction on a three-story, gopherwood ark?

My guess is that Noah had to field more than one insult, slur, and perhaps worse as his work went on. If this were you, where would your grace under pressure come from? How would you keep calm so that others would not panic? How did Noah do it?

There is nothing in Genesis to indicate that Noah crumbled under the pressure. Nor do we ever hear that he argued with God, "A boat? All of this will fit in a boat?" or rejected God's time frame, "Can't this happen in a few more years? Or maybe never?"

Amazingly, too, he didn't seem to doubt himself as the one to take the leadership role. "But I have to feed my family." And he didn't fall back on his age, either. "But, I'm six hundred years old!"—which, we're told in Genesis, he was at the time the floods came.

This steadfastness shines with the Spirit and trust in God, forged from deep and regular prayer and an outward life of goodness—a wonderful example for us whenever we're faced with a monumental problem. With inner strength, we can execute any, even monumental, plan.

The days unfolded as God said they would. Noah made sure that the ark was constructed to God's specification. Then he herded his family and the animals inside when the time came and pulled up the walkway. Safe inside with his loved ones, he could be assured that things thus far had worked according to God's plan, so there was hope for the future, too. The ark might pitch from side to side with the rising floodwaters, but physically he was safe, and spiritually he was reassured. The storm wore on, a disaster for the earth, to be sure. But this time, for Noah, what could have been a crisis was actually a validation of God's promise and plan to him, a good man.

In our own lives, when we're faced with a crisis, often our minds will whirl with questions, doubt, and worry. If we have a good habit of deep breathing, spiritually and physically, we can calm some of that agitation with quiet, prayerful stillness. When we've diminished the noise in our hearts, we can get a better understanding of what resources we have to tackle our problem, and from that place of possibility, we can move ahead, filling in the gaps of our needs as we go. When we resist the many temptations in the world around us, we can further strengthen ourselves and be ready for any crisis to come.

FAITH IN FOCUS

Think about a crisis that you have faced. What resources were most helpful for you, especially personal attributes and talents? What resources held you back? Make a note to increase your beneficial resources and work on or minimize those that were not helpful. Have faith that you will do even better the next time.

_____

_____

_____

_____

_____

_____

Keeping Faith, Finding Patience

Of course, once Noah and everyone else were in the ark, trouble did not evaporate. Torrential flood waters engulfed the earth, and the rains fell for forty days.

Forty days!

And Genesis tells us that Noah was six hundred years old when the floodwaters came (Genesis 7:6), not a young man with a perceived long life ahead of him. Imagine if you were older, as Noah was, and you're hearing driving rain on your roof for forty days. And you are confined in a relatively small space with pairs of every creature that had walked or flown on earth—and your family, too.

Cozy and companionable? Or something else entirely?

After the rains, the flood waters stayed high and fatal to everyone and everything except Noah and the other inhabitants of the ark—for another 150 days! Still, all inhabitants of the ark were bobbing along together.

Imagine how you would be feeling about then. And then…

You have to wait another several months, when the ark comes to rest on a mountain, and the waters begin to recede!

I have often heard people bemoan their lack of patience. I do that sometimes, too, especially when I'm eager for something to happen or a difficult time is stretching on for way too long. I know that patience is a virtue, but it's oh so difficult to find it when I most need it!

Again, today's society often runs counter to our having patience. We're quite the instant civilization—everything from food to streaming films, everything is so much more quickly available than at any other time in the world's history.

If we have to wait for long for anything, we feel stress rising within— a sure sign that impatience is getting the upper hand. And when we are impatient, we can lose our temper, act rashly, harm ourselves or others, or make a mess of that which we wanted to turn out well.

Impatience can lead us back to the darker side of what-if speculation and prompt us to act on rising anxiety and, perhaps, panic. How do we avoid this? Gain more patience? Know when it is right to act (and know what to do) in a situation that drags on for days or months?

Quiet. Prayer. Assessment of resources at hand. Understanding of where you are in the situation (the life cycle of a crisis), and what is going on inside of you—these tools that you have been working on are very important, now. Instead of a knee jerk reaction, you need to still cultivate that kneeling-down reaction of breathing, slowing your stress response, and listening in stillness to help you act from a place of calm and solid knowledge.

Noah, being human and in a very tight situation, seems to have had a battle with impatience. After months and months in the ark, and with the waters receding, he sends out a raven to see if the land is dry enough so that they can all leave the ark in safety. Did he think, "Oh, it has to be all-clear now. Maybe God just forgot to tell me." We don't hear, at this point, any pronouncement from God that it is safe to leave.

Or did Noah's patience run out, and he thought, as we might have, "Enough. We're on a dry mountain, so there must be other dry land around, so let's all leave this ark and get on with living"? Crisis solved? Well, it wouldn't have been if he'd done that, because the raven did not find adequate dry land. Nor did a dove, which Noah dispatched after the raven returned.

Can you imagine how agonizing it must have been for Noah and his family, waiting and waiting for the crisis to fully play itself out, and the earth to be habitable again? It must have taken tremendous will-power and prayer to stay on the ark for all that time!

Finally, of course, Noah sends out another dove, and this one returns with a broken-off olive branch to signify it was safe to leave the ark, and the earth was repeopled and reinhabited again. But if Noah had given into his oh-so-human impatience, the trajectory of the Bible and, indeed, the world, would have been very different.

Never an Inventory of Nothing

Noah was lucky: God gave him details. Unfortunately for most of us in a crisis, we will probably not get something quite as precise. So in our time between crises, sometimes we expand on what-ifs by looking at what we perceive to be as lacking in our world, and we let that jump into the worrisome stew of stress bubble over into panic. Often, these thoughts arrive unannounced, when we are relaxed and ready for bed. Suddenly, our minds begin to spin over problems that have yet to happen (if they ever do) and relate them to what we lack:

• Money. "What if something happened to my husband, and I couldn't keep the roof over our heads?"

• Connections. "What if my grandmother has cancer, and I can't find the right doctors for her?"

• Safety. "What if my identity is stolen again, and my credit is ruined for good?"

• Resources. "What if, because of my job, I have to move the family across country, and they don't want to go?"

If we think in terms of *necessary, possible, impossible,* these and other problems of resources can be chipped away at.

First, necessary: Turn each worry around to "What *is*...?"

• Money: What is my financial situation, and as a parent do I have insurance and other safety mechanisms in place (a will, durable power of attorney, etc.) in case something happens to me?

• Connections: What doctors are in my grandmother's network, and would it be possible to request a referral outside of it, if she needs one?

• Safety: What is the status of my credit? Am I protected against identity theft, and have I set up free credit-monitoring? If not, can I do this, even if I have to pay for it?

• Resources: What is my job status? How does my family feel about the possibility of moving? Do I have skills that would translate to another job so we could stay where we are?

As you identify the need specifically, posing questions that you can act upon, you will have turned a nebulous worry into positive steps you can take to better protect yourself and loved ones. Moreover, you can take these actions before a crisis strikes and you discover that you're not prepared! Allow this peace of mind to ease you into sleep, lessen your stress, and affirm that you need not feel like a victim. You need not panic. But be sure to protect your action points from further what-ifs, such as, "Oh, my, I don't have enough insurance; what happens if something happens before I arrange to have more?"

Make a firm resolution to not revisit the what-ifs and stick to it, enlisting the help of your loved ones, if need be.

Second, focus on the possible. Start gathering tangible resources, reach out to people you know, find places to go for help, and make use of the talents you have inside of you. Find that insurance, talk to that doctor, and get answers for those worries that have pulled you down into anxiety. Keep a list or a log of everything you are doing and finding out. Each time you feel anxiety begin to bubble up, revisit your list, read it carefully, and allow a better sense of calm to come over you as you realize you are not helpless.

Third, by turning a what-if to what is, you can now begin to act, doing what you thought previously was impossible. You can use your God-given creative mind and many inner talents to good purpose and with good result. And you will have set the stage for an easier time, next time. When next you worry, rely on the three-part framework to guide you out of what-ifs to what is and onward to a feeling of greater control in a more positive outcome, no matter what happens.

FAITH IN FOCUS

Write in your journal of a difficult time when you felt you had no control. What emotions did you express? What did you do? Now, write what you learned from that time. Consider how you would be better able to handle a similar situation again. Have faith that you are able to learn from past experiences and turn those lessons into strong, proactive steps to feel better control moving forward.

_____

_____

_____

_____

_____

_____

A Contemporary Lesson

Moving from dark what-if scenarios to what-is possibilities not only brings solutions to thorny problems, but gives you greater hope in tomorrow. I learned this many years ago, from a young child who, if you looked only at the superficial, would have seemingly not had many resources at all to help him.

I enjoy writing and producing children's theater, especially musicals. A number of years ago, one of my plays, *What Do You Want to Be When You Grow Up?* toured some of the schools in Los Angeles. It had a simple premise: through comedy and improvisation, two characters engaged with the children about what they wanted to be and what it would take for them to get there (school, skills, etc.).

After the performance at one inner-city elementary school, I joined the actors to continue speaking with the children about their life dreams. One little boy in particular impressed me; he was smaller than most of the other boys but was sitting perfectly still and straight in his chair, listening to everything that was being said. As the questions wound down, I looked at him and asked, "What about you? What would you like to be when you grow up?"

Suddenly, he all but collapsed. Shoulders stooped, eyes on the floor, arms folded, his soft voice was clipped, as if the words didn't belong to him. He said, "I can't be anything. There's nothing I can do."

Intuitively, I thought he must have heard that from someone, probably an adult, who was absolutely mean, even abusive. I felt a ripple of anger in me; who would have planted that horrible seed of doubt in someone so very young? Granted, the boy's surroundings were not very uplifting, but there were positives: The teachers and administrators seemed to be very bright and caring, and the classrooms were well-kept and well-stocked with books and supplies.

I was going to say, "Oh, don't say that," but something stopped me—that small, quiet voice inside that I try to cultivate through daily prayer and silence. So instead of speaking right away, I prayed for wisdom. It was just a split second of prayer, but I am ever so thankful I did!

"Oh, I think there's a lot you could do," I said, "You really paid attention during the show, and you look strong and intelligent. And you spoke up just now. Yes, I think there's a lot you could do."

His shoulders straightened a little, and he looked at me and blinked.

"Now, what is it you would *like* to do?" I asked him, with a smile. His words tumbled out in a rush. "I want to be a football player, a basketball player, and a fireman!"

"That's great!" I told him, and then the actors and I talked about the importance of training and other things those professionals do to prepare for their careers. We were fully aware that the likelihood of the boy making it to the professional ranks was slim, as it would be for any child aspiring to a career as an athlete. But the point was: where before there had been hopelessness, now there was hope and a spark of determination that needed to be encouraged so it would grow into something achievable and good.

After the show and discussion, a teacher pulled me aside. "That boy, he comes from a very tough home," she told me. "But I really like how you handled him just now. We can work with that."

I thanked God that I'd allowed myself to listen and took that mindful, prayerful moment. My anger at why I thought the boy had initially answered the way he did could have clouded my ability to respond in a way that would be helpful. Then, I thanked God that he would have teachers who now knew to support him even more, coaching him in finding his God-given talents and develop those, even if he didn't have many other, external resources to call upon.

Just as breathing is a tool for stress relief and resilience readily at our disposal, we have internal talents and gifts that form the basis for what we can do in any given crisis or difficult situation. The better we know what these are and nurture them, the more we will find them useful in times of challenge. That knowledge will also help us trust, maintain patience, and find hope as the world and circumstances around us seem very dire, perhaps even doubtful.

We might not know what is to come, but if we embrace the necessary and understand and nurture the possible, we can be well on our way to meeting the challenge of the impossible—and inspiring others to do so, too!

CHAPTER FOUR

Never Alone

There is nothing on this earth more to be prized than true friendship.
—attributed to St. Thomas Aquinas

Despite all of the skills we bring to challenging times in our lives, we never operate through them in a vacuum. We always come in contact with, need, and benefit from other people.

Some of these men and women are familiar, perhaps even family members. Others are complete strangers. All can be our "angels on earth," true treasure in our lives—if we recognize them for who they are, the gifts they bring, and nurture the ties, however slight, that we share with them.

The Value of Friendship

It might seem odd to quote a doctor of the church and master theologian at the beginning of a chapter about the place and importance of good people in our lives, especially friends. For many people today, St. Thomas Aquinas is known perhaps only for his tremendous intellect and authorship of the *Summa Theologica*. But Thomas recognized, as so many before and after him did, that a good life necessarily calls for and involves communication and relationships with others.

I'm not a Thomist scholar, but still I find much in his writing to inform us today, especially about the crucial role of others in our lives. For Thomas, people could no more be isolated from others than from God. The good within each of us is to be put forth for the good of all, and we need good friends to do this.

Today, the context for the many of the words St. Thomas uses, such as *true* and *friend*, might be understood differently, but still, there is a familiar underlying understanding. I especially like the following passage from the *Summa*, "Whether the Fellowship of Friends Is Necessary for Happiness?":

> If we speak of the happiness of this life, the happy man needs friends, as the Philosopher says, not, indeed, to make use of them, since he suffices himself; nor to delight in them, since he possesses perfect delight in the operation of virtue; but for the purpose of a good operation, viz. that he may do good to them; that he may delight in seeing them do good; and again that he may be helped by them in his good work. For in order that man may do well, whether in the works of the active life, or in those of the contemplative life, he needs to have the fellowship of friends.[6]

And, of course, not just any friends. Thomas is very particular about writing of "good" in people and in society, good that is for the benefit of all and springs from the good within us. That same good that we nurture when we take those deep spiritual breaths and drive away distraction so we can get to the beautiful soul beneath. With good others, friends include spouse, children, other family members, nonrelated friends, and also strangers who are, themselves, intent on doing good for us and with us. Together we can strengthen each other spiritually and emotionally, guarding ourselves from that which is not good in the world. We steel ourselves against crises, or if catastrophes occur, we have a first-rate support system to help us and a wonderful opportunity to help others when they need us, too.

With good friends, true friends, I also believe we can lessen or eliminate any panic that we might have; with people around us who care and are ready to help, we can loosen the anxiety that we have to do everything ourselves. Worry and those dark clouds over our heads can be talked through and prayed out with good friends. The assurance of a hug, a presence, a kind word can be greater balm than any lock on the door!

True Friends

The support of friends, especially in times of crisis, is vital to helping us through the emotions that flood and fuel our hearts. From serving as sounding boards to offering a shoulder to cry on, true friends will not cower if we express our emotions, giving vent to our sorrow, anger, fear, and even despair. They will help us see clearly enough to move through mourning, provide lighter moments, too, especially if we might seem to teeter on the edge of truly losing hope. They will be the personification of God's unconditional love and help us find even greater spiritual depth.

Far from the world of theological apologetics and as a validation for what many of us already know in our hearts to be true, science has dived into the subject of friends (social support) and how they relate to better workplace environments, stress reduction, security, and safety. Even a superficial survey on the benefits of a social support system and health reveals a variety of studies, including one on how social networks had a protective factor on older African Americans who experienced discrimination[7] and one that found that social support from the boss of a group of firefighters in Alicante, Spain, had a "mediating role of resilience" on the firefighters who faced "intense emotional demands" on the job.[8]

Still other studies highlight the importance of a strong social support system throughout life, but especially in the golden years when health and other factors can be especially challenging. And at least once around Valentine's Day or in the wedding month of June, there is a news report (or two) that says that married people and those that live with a loved one tend to live longer and be happier!

We might be inclined to say, "Why are they spending money and valuable time on studies like these when the results seem so obvious?" But there can be good, practical reasons for trying to quantify or better understand in a scientific way human behavior and what is beneficial to overall well-being.

If a theory has solid science to back it up, physicians and other medical professionals will be more likely to fold it into their practice, and ultimately, patients will benefit from it. Also, these and other studies help highlight which populations might be most in need of assistance. They also might show what kind of assistance is most effective (for example, a direct supervisor's support might be more effective than one more distant when it comes to helping a team of firefighters deal with the stresses of their jobs).

But even with theological, personal, and scientific arguments championing the necessity and benefits of friendship, we still face a major impediment to enjoying this simple, powerful asset in our lives. Today's world is increasingly becoming anything but encouraging of true, good, close relationships, just as it is becoming more difficult to breathe healthfully.

Difficult, yes. But not impossible—if we prepare the proverbial ground with fertile, friendly soil.

The Problem of True Friendship

Before we can have true, strong friends, we have to find and cultivate them. This requires a blend of skills that include quality communication, attentive listening, focused presence, and the ability to encourage, perceive, and appreciate the other person for who he or she is. It also requires sharing values. It is very difficult to have a close, true friend who is on a completely different moral page than you are, because not just ideas, but actions spring from the values we hold. To me, a close friend is one on whom I could count to act as I morally would, should I be unable to do so myself.

Sadly, the art of nurturing friendships—encouraging, and sustaining good-quality relationships that are uplifting for all concerned—is making its way to the endangered list. I don't say this idly because I have noticed how isolated individuals in society are becoming, and how I sometimes get pulled in, too, by the tendency to cocoon.

As we gaze more into screens of one kind or another—friend to friend, spouse to spouse, even doctor to patient—we diminish human relating that can open up worlds of natural understanding. And as we use technology to shop, eat (those delivery services are convenient), and chat, we diminish the contact we have even more, and the intuitive aspect of communicating can atrophy.

And, oh my, have we totally blurred or, perhaps, eliminated the distinction between *friend* and *acquaintance*, lumping nearly everyone with whom we have any e-time into the former category! For example, friends and acquaintances may both send pictures from their vacations, but true friends will tell us how they felt, what was behind the pictures. Acquaintances will collect us into their network of "friends" but seldom reach out personally to us and engage us in meaningful dialogue. True friends will take time, attention, and personalize their time with us. Acquaintances may tell us they will pray for us if we're sick, but true friends will be the ones offering help, no matter the hour! Yet both of these categories of relationship seem to meld into one as we throw our thoughts and activities out openly to a long list of names.

Another challenge today is, of course, time. Good friends take time to nurture—if you think of how long it's taken you to better understand yourself, then you have a sense of the enormity of the time commitment! But with all of our other responsibilities, it can be nearly impossible to find that good time for a good friend. And yet it is so vital to take that time—in the long run, you won't need your job to share your successes and joys with, and you won't need your hobby to help you through a devastating period in life—but you will need your true friends.

FAITH IN FOCUS

Of all the people whom you know, who are your closest friends? Which of these would you most rely on to help in times of crisis? Do you spend most of your available relationship time cultivating and caring for these people, these true friends? Is there someone other than these people whose relationship could be that of a true friend, but you are neglecting it? Why or why not? Resolve to care for your true friends, and those who should be (perhaps a neglected spouse or other relative). Have faith that, as these relationships become even stronger, your life will benefit from the good you all share.

An Invitation to Share Vision, Values, Life

So, how do you find these angels on earth? These true friends? And how do you keep these precious relationships going through all the changes in life? Reinventing the wheel is not necessary. When you think of a true friend, you probably already have someone specific in mind, perhaps more than one person. So you know the physical ways you can encounter a friend.

You might have met a good friend through school, work, or a recreational activity. Perhaps you forged a friendship during a crisis and stayed in touch, building on the bonds you developed during trying times. Maybe, through a gradual realization, or even a sudden moment, you found a friend in someone you had taken for granted or forgotten in your haste to make more flashy friends.

Your best friend could be the spouse with whom you share a home and family, but whose life seems to run in parallel to your equally busy one.

A true friend could be the young son or daughter you care for now, but who later becomes a wonderful adult who advocates for you as you enter the last days of your life.

The best of friendships, true friends whom we invite into the most personal level of our lives, are those who want good for us and bring out good in ourselves and themselves. These precious relationships thrive on the fertile ground of shared visions and values. True friends are not found by casting a wide net and reeling in hundreds. They are invited into our lives through the prism of our spiritual vision, personal values, and life character. This we know not only from observing people in our own lives, but from stellar examples in the past.

Can you imagine Jesus without his disciples? Gandhi without thousands of like-minded Indians, and especially his close circle of supporters? St. Francis without his band of brothers, or Blessed Mother Teresa of Calcutta without her sisters?

Can you imagine your life without your loved ones, your true friends? History would not have been the same. Your life, my life, today would not be the same without those precious people to enhance, challenge, and encourage us.

We can see through the examples of Jesus, Gandhi, St. Francis, and Mother Teresa that there is great depth to the bonds that tie people together to weather adversity and achieve great things. There are also, as with any human relationships, challenges.

Jesus's disciples were a varied group of men—a tax collector, fishermen, others from different backgrounds. But all were intent on following Christ and, especially, learning from him. Throughout the New Testament, we see them ask questions, offer answers, seek truth, and then desire to spread that truth to others. This is a shared vision, a common desire, and it kept them close to Jesus to the end and beyond.

This is not to say that Jesus had smooth sailing always with his disciples. Sometimes, as in the Garden of Gethsemane on the night of the Last Supper, Jesus had to coach them, truly wake them up to what he needed from them. Still, their shared vision did not evaporate, not even as the ultimate crisis—Jesus's death on the cross—shook them to the core. True friends are found in many places, but all will come together in a crisis—even if they need a bit of coaching to know how!

St. Francis joyfully welcomed fellow brothers, true friends, to join him in his ministry; even with his deep and personal spiritual life and practice, he seemed to take delight in having others to share the life with him, and to share their common values. Sometimes, Francis feared that the brothers might falter, step away from the poverty and full-focus dedication of the mission. But he could take time, reflecting in his cave retreat, and find renewed enthusiasm for the journey and infuse his brothers with that light and joy, putting them firmly back on track. True friends rejoice in common work and play but also expect one another to give an occasional reality check, when need be.

When Mahatma Gandhi arrived in South Africa in 1893 and began his journey to peacefully achieve rights for colored people (the term used at that time to mean non-Caucasian people), he was met with heartfelt support from the local Indians who were suffering from oppression. But he soon discovered that many of those who would help him were not quite equipped to do so. They had the heart, but they did not all possess the developed resources to make an individual and collective difference.[9] Gandhi determined what was needed and even rolled up his sleeves and taught English so that more Indians could actively rally and express their views. He encouraged them, coaxing out of them inner gifts that translated clearly as the days of peaceful struggle wore on and, eventually, bore fruit. His approach was not one of condescension, but respect and love, and a desire to give tools that he himself prized. True friends want to seek personal development and growth—and will gratefully accept wisdom and instruction from one another to do so.

For Blessed Mother Teresa of Calcutta to carry out her God-given mission, she needed others around her and out in the world beyond. But hers was not an easy mission, nor was her invitation without demands. She was firm in her commitment and in what that commitment meant for the person who might join her. Work, entire and selfless, was necessary, no posturing for camera crews and fame. She chose, by staying true to her principles, true friends who were strong enough to face harsh realities with her, alongside her. True friends respect one another's goals and work—and allow goodness to grow and flourish through common affection and labor.

The Invitation for Strangers

Sometimes, despite our true, close friends, we still might feel alone, particularly at vulnerable times, when a crisis has just occurred. Alone in the doctor's office, in our totaled car, in the late night when the telephone rings, we sense beyond the physical lack of someone a gnawing anxiety that we're going to have to face trouble by ourselves— and we fear we are not up to the task.

At those times, I have found it helps to remember that the invitation to goodness and nurturing good, to welcoming angels on earth, extends beyond those we know to those whom we do not know. For example, if the crisis concerns health, our angel on earth might be

- the pharmacist who double-checks the prescriptions
- the lab tech who runs the tests
- the scheduler who seemingly moves heaven and earth to make way for us when we need an unexpected doctor's appointment
- the nurse who looks into the examination room while we're waiting for the doctor, sees us crying, and takes a moment to comfort us

These and other men and woman handle very personal information; they might even know more about us than our close family members and friends do! Yet we might never know their names, where they live, their family situations, or anything else that's personal. They talk us through intricate procedures or paperwork, but we usually do not know what they look like or how old they are—or if they have had the procedures themselves. They often enter our lives at highly emotional times but do not stay, moving on after their piece of the puzzle is in place.

Beyond the healthcare arena, in other crisis-driven situations, we encounter these anonymous helpers. A call to 911 results in an entire team of anonymous firefighters responding to a house ablaze. A loved one dies, and a group of employees at the mortuary, whom you do not know, carry out preparations for the funeral service. A church-based congregation takes up a collection for the poor, donating money to a homeless shelter, and individuals are housed and fed as a result.

They are everywhere, these angels on earth, and oh so often, we take them for granted or let that stubbornness prevent us from seeing their worth. Part of this blindness occurs when we're deep in a crisis and in pain, overwhelmed by the things we have to do. We think, "I am all alone in this." We let that feeling sink in, and we might wallow in it, pulled under by the darkness of the situation. Yes, we might believe we are alone.

But, the truth is, we never are. Moreover, these people provide us with the important opportunity to be a friend in return, to cultivate goodness even with a stranger.

FAITH IN FOCUS

Who are the strangers who helped you today? How did you respond to them? If you were encouraging and uplifting, how did they respond back to you? What about if you were abrupt? Angry or irritated? Think about the strangers you might meet tomorrow and how you might bring out the good in them and the situation surrounding your encounter. Have faith that, as you call upon your deep spiritual reservoir, you can foster good feelings and a good outcome.

_____

_____

_____

_____

_____

_____

A breath before speaking, a prayer before responding—these and other small "moments" can ease at least some of the anger, impatience, or fear that you might feel while waiting (how hard it is to maintain calm when those irritating songs on hold loop over and over again), explaining yourself over and over again, or otherwise repeating yourself to the point where you feel as if you are spinning your wheels. Then, a kind word when you finally do connect with a live person can make all the difference between a productive, successful encounter and a disastrous one.

I found this to be absolutely the case when I lived through a string of crises in the spring of 2013. From May to June of that year, I was diagnosed with a very painful, inoperable arthritis in both of my knees and had to change many aspects of my lifestyle, including movements and activities; I was hit by a car that ran a red light, and my left arm was injured; and my father died.

One of these events would have been quite enough for a year, but all three in such quick succession very nearly took the proverbial wind out of my sails! I tried to tend to the possible, trying to be especially gentle on my body so that pain would not be overwhelming. But with each blow, my resilience frayed, and it became easier to cry often and on very little provocation.

I don't know what I would have done without the help, moral support, and outpouring of prayer and care from my friends, including my mother! When I needed someone to listen, I only had to reach out. When I needed a ride to a doctor's appointment, my friends stepped up. And without even asking, I knew that people were petitioning God and covering me in comfort, wisdom, and strength.

Beyond the support of friends, I also enjoyed tremendous support from my doctors, including their staffs, insurance agents and other employees, and a host of other angels who helped ease the practical matters that went along with each of the three crises. I could not begin to name each of them, but all along the way, I tried to encourage, appreciate, and thank as many as I could. I found that the more I extended gratitude, the easier it was to deal with all the glitches that arose. And the more I tried to cultivate goodness around me, the more goodness grew.

With all of that support, I felt lifted and protected. Although I might become frustrated or worn down, I knew that I wasn't going to fall into thoughts of hopelessness or expectation that another shoe would drop just around the corner.

Yes, even with great spiritual resilience, we do not navigate crises alone.

Indeed, through each crisis I've experienced, and the relatively calm times, too, I cannot say enough in gratitude and praise for my very true friends and family. What security to know that there will be someone who can help (and be helped in return), someone who understands (and who is understood), and someone who can laugh, cry, and praise along with me! And what a profoundly good way to eliminate much of the dark, worrisome overtones of life—no better way to cast off what is not good than to spend time enjoying the company of those who are good.

The Other Side of True Friendship

If wonderful friendship nurtures good in and around us, then is the opposite also true? What about those friends who might even be in our immediate circle, but they are not helpful, kind, or compassionate when we need them to be? What about those who try to undermine us and the good we feel or wish to do?

What about people who are hypercritical of us or make us more stressed, even if they try to be helpful and caring? Or the people who somehow seem to sap our energies and time, commodities that are extremely short-supplied during a crisis (or at other times, too, if you have other serious responsibilities or an ongoing illness or disability).

When I was first diagnosed with lupus, a wise rabbi advised me to avoid toxic people. He understood the need to be compassionate and forgiving, and to regard others with fundamental respect. However, he told me, "Just as you wouldn't want to fill your body with toxic substances, you shouldn't fill your heart and soul with toxic people."

I went away from that conversation a bit confused. Newly diagnosed, all of my friends had offered their sympathy and help. However, as the days and months wore on, and lupus and other conditions continued to be fiercely active, some of these friends began to fall away or chafe at my sickness-weary spirit. Some encouraged me to throw caution aside and just live as I had before. To them, I didn't look sick (many people with lupus actually look very healthy, while the disease is causing great damage internally), so they couldn't accept that I had limitations. Others made unreasonable demands on my mental energy and time, so precious in the face of awful fatigue.

Some Christians told me that I was not faithful enough, that my illness was a punishment. At the time, these remarks seemed frightfully mean and misinformed. The God in whom I believe and have faith is a loving God, and not one who visits harsh things upon us, including illness. But as I came to understand, even within the most faithful flock, there can be people who misinterpret the Word, or superimpose their own, wrong-hearted ideas on that which is true.

Yes, as wonderful as it is to enjoy a community of believers and to benefit from their support, even there, sometimes, we can encounter toxicity.

FAITH IN FOCUS

Are there people in your life who might be toxic to your spiritual and emotional health? Do you feel helpless to control their influence or repel their negative impact? Try to lessen the time you spend with any toxic people in your life. Build up a spirit that can pray for them to change while, at the same time, protecting yourself from their influence. Have faith that, as you spend more time with good people and in good spiritual practice, you will lessen the impact of toxicity.

Daniel X. Freedman Professor of Psychiatry in the David Geffen School of Medicine at UCLA, Margaret L. Stuber, MD, recognizes the strong and often positive influence a faith and a faith community can have on its members. I spoke with her after reading an interview she gave in a magazine published by UCLA. In that interview, she says, "I often wish I could just prescribe faith to people."[10] She repeated this incredibly wise—and obvious!—statement when we spoke.

A religious belief system, Dr. Stuber said, can help someone in crisis feel secure that "somehow this all makes sense," even if it is impossible to know exactly how, such as the Catholic faith's recognition of mystery. But she added, "Separate from that is the sense of spirituality, which may coexist with the community in an ideal world. However, some people may be in a community and not have a deep inner sense of connectedness."

"Social support with a community of believers, a formal religion or group that meditates together, can be extremely helpful to people," said Dr. Stuber. "But, it can be hard when the religious belief system supposes that, 'if I do good works, I get rewarded, if I do bad things, I get punished.' It can be destructive for people."

How do we handle those other people, who, unfortunately, might pose as being helpful but are trying to scam us when we are most vulnerable—those up to no good at all, even if they might be close to us, in our families, social circle, or faith or spirit community?

St. Thomas Aquinas had some thoughts about this very question: "Since true friendship is based on virtue, whatever there is contrary to virtue in a friend is an obstacle to friendship, and whatever in him is virtuous is an incentive to friendship."[11] Thus, could a friend who desires less than good for us be a true friend?

Not likely.

The life of another saint—St. Augustine—serves as an example of someone who, early on, was influenced by seemingly good friends, but they did not have his best interests at heart. In his deeply personal and moving autobiography, *The Confessions*, he writes of the influence of his father, who took pride in Augustine's intellect and physical development, and of his friends, about whom he said,

> I ran headlong with such great blindness that I was ashamed to be remiss in vice in the midst of my comrades. For I heard them boast of their disgraceful acts, and glory in them all the more, the more debased they were…. But lest I be put to scorn, I made myself more depraved than I was…I pretended that I had done what I had not done, lest I be considered more contemptible because I was actually more innocent, and lest I be held a baser thing because more chaste than the others.[12]

This desire to live up to the "debased" acts and standards of friends took an early toll on Augustine's spiritual self. For years, he continued on the same road, and that toll weighed more heavily with each step away from the goodness within him. Even when he thought he was turning to God, the group he fell in with was comprised of "certain men, doting in their pride, too carnal-minded and glib of speech, in whose mouth were the snares of the devil and a very birdlime confected by mixing together the syllables of your name and the name of our Lord Jesus Christ, and the name of the Paraclete, our comforter, the Holy Spirit."[13]

Augustine's life could have been but one more regular citizen of his time, come and gone with no record. But his was a strong spirit, and aside from his cadre of spiritually harmful friends, he had other, better champions on his side, especially his mother, whom we now know as St. Monica. As long as Augustine's internal goodness was at odds with how he felt and how he should be acting (and at odds with those with whom he surrounded himself—a true crisis of the soul), his search for God continued. It was a years-long, spiritually deep breath, but eventually, the crisis resolved, and Augustine's innate sense of goodness won.

The Confessions is a monumental testament to how we might set ourselves down the wrong path with the wrong people and mire ourselves in life-shattering crises as a result. However, if we continue to seek good in God and others, our connection with the Spirit inside us can become stronger, and we can find our souls filled with light, rather than darkness. In this world, plagued with troubles, we will lessen the negative, harmful, and stressful influences that come at us from seemingly all sides as we cultivate goodness and spiritual strength. The more we emphasize the positive in our lives, our wonderful true friends, and the love that they give us and we give them, the more prepared we will be when the awful happens and a crisis erupts.

CHAPTER FIVE

Into the Fire

Your husband suffers a stroke, and your world is turned upside down as you realize that you will now be caregiver, breadwinner, and sole parent to your children.

You arrive home after a wonderful evening out with friends to see fire trucks outside the charred shell of your house and suddenly realize that you are homeless.

A split second of distraction causes you to turn the wrong way down a side street, and you cause a collision with an oncoming car that claims the life of the other driver.

Flooding engulfs your town, and not only is your life forever changed, but so is that of everyone you have called neighbor and all you have known as familiar.

You may not know when it's going to happen. You might not know what it will be. But inevitably, sometime, somehow, you will be faced with a crisis that will demand all of your attention, strength, courage, and wisdom—and then demand more. For these life-changing and often life-defining moments, you don't have time to say, "Wait a minute. I'm not ready for this!" or, "I'd like to turn the clock back a few hours and approach this situation differently."

No, at that moment, you are in it, and there's no turning back.

As you move into the fire that will refine you and define your life, at least for a time, the tools you have within you will be invaluable supports. Your preparedness, including the things I have spoken about in previous chapters—good and true friends and physical, emotional, and spiritual deep breathing—will enable you to be less frightened and better able to assist others while keeping your center in God's Spirit protected and strong. You will also be able to identify where you can be even stronger, or discover new talents you never realized you possessed.

Yes, crises can bring out the best of us in the worst of situations. Here are three situations from my own experience to illustrate what I mean.

A Crisis Trilogy

The 1990s were some of the most difficult years of my life, punctuated by many crises that have had a profound impact on who I am today and why I felt called to write this book. Death and loss, natural disasters and civil unrest, health crises and personal upheaval, the 1990s certainly had it all, starting with the firestorm ignited by the Rodney King verdict in 1992.

On Wednesday, April 29, 1992, a jury in Simi Valley, California, acquitted four white police officers in the beating of black motorist Rodney King. The racial descriptions are important, here, as this was the catalyst that sparked the beginning of protest and violence that spread through many sections of Los Angeles, where I live, on the day following the trial.

I was near South Los Angeles (at the time, it was known as South-Central Los Angeles), not far from the area that became the center of the violence, driving home from a conference, when I heard on the radio about the verdict. I immediately felt that trouble could erupt close by. So I suspect, did many others on the roads that afternoon; traffic became thicker and thicker, slower and slower.

It's difficult to describe the feeling of vulnerability that crept into my heart during that drive. Alone in my car, I listened to the radio and started to hear the first troubling reports of unrest brewing. I had the sense that there was little to separate me from anything that might happen—no way to quickly race away. So I prayed and kept vigilant and, thank the Lord, arrived home safely. There, I turned on my television and watched the unfolding of the Los Angeles riots.

I had a very personal connection to South Los Angeles at that time. I was the director of an African American gospel choir at a Catholic Church in the area. As I saw the news reports of businesses being looted and torched, cars being attacked, and people dying, I became increasingly fearful for the people I held dear in areas near where the trouble seemed to be concentrated. I stayed up far into the night, praying as the situation worsened.

The next morning, I awoke to the smell of something bitter oozing through my apartment windows. I looked out and saw a murky pall hanging in the air; smoke from fires set in the wake of the verdicts was being hemmed in by the moist marine layer. Although my neighborhood was unaffected by the rioting, there was no way to escape the smell and the feel of what was happening just a few miles away.

That first full day of the unrest, businesses, including the one I was working in, opened as usual. However, at the office where I worked, the day was anything but regular, as we tried to keep apprised of events that moved rapidly and deteriorated in several parts of Los Angeles. The violence spread, the National Guard was called in, and my sense of vulnerability increased as the city fell under siege.

FOCUS ON FAITH

Have you ever lived through a crisis fueled by hatred or a severe misunderstanding? How did you respond? How did you feel? What dynamics worked to increase the tension in the situation? How might you have worked to bring greater calm or peace to those involved, especially the innocent or the victims? Have faith that your experience has imparted a valuable lesson, one that you can use in the future, should you again be confronted by hate or misunderstandings.

At that point, I feared not only for the people in my choir, their families, and our church and pastor, but also for all innocent people, white, black, Korean, Japanese, Chinese, Mexican, or other, whose lives were being forced into such an environment by a relatively small group of people, many of whom, we learned later, were taking advantage of the situation to loot, rob, set fires, and commit other crimes.

Shortly after lunch, the authorities asked businesses in our area to close, so that the National Guard and other law enforcement could move more freely through the streets. But immediately after the request, traffic spilled out so quickly onto the streets that roads and intersections were clogged and barely snailing along. I had no choice but to join the long line of vehicles idling in the streets—and remember the feeling of the day before, when I'd just learned of the verdicts in similar, bumper-to-bumper traffic!

The Federal Building, a government office complex, was two blocks from my office. It had become a magnet for protesters and others whose motives were, to me, hazy; at one intersection, a man on foot and dressed in a white robe with a large cross on the front and a white hood snaked his way through the cars, passing right in front of me as he headed for a group of protesters on a far corner. Again, that sense of acute vulnerability resurfaced like a queasiness rising in my throat.

My two-and-a-half-mile drive home took a nerve-wracking three and a half hours!

Back home, I waited. Waited for the trouble to stop. Waited for word from my friends. Waited on God's peace and calm for my heart and the city.

One of the most unnerving parts of a crisis is having to wait. There are often so many factors we do not control, and our creative minds can spin all sorts of theories and what-if scenarios to fill in the gaping blanks of the unfinished story.

As the LA riots wore on, one of the things that I began to worry greatly about was the impact of the unrest on racial relations in the months and years to come. Not just the overall, citywide implications, but the deeply personal implications of my relationship with the people in my choir and the parish at St. Eugene. I had come to love being a part of the unabashed, joy-filled spiritual fellowship, and my faith had deepened greatly through the gospel music and vitality of the church. It was an unusual situation, to be sure; the other African American Catholic gospel choir directors in Los Angeles were men of color. But through music and the Church tradition, I had found open hearts and true friends. As racial conflict escalated in those days of unrest, I feared that somehow my experience with the choir would be deeply affected, too.

And it was, but in a blessedly positive way!

As I have learned again and again, a creative mind can be warped by what-if gloom, but it is by praying through those dark moments and by relying on true loved ones that we can turn our focus to the good side of the result.

Ultimately, it was God, through his Spirit in the members of the choir, that cut through the fear and anxiety. We did not have an evening rehearsal that week, but several of us kept in touch, covering the entire situation with prayers for peace, compassion, understanding, and hope. There is no doubt in my mind that those prayers and that fellowship brought more security and peace than any armed presence could. It certainly made me realize how profound a resource is prayer shared by others, especially in an unsteady, upended world. No matter what color we are, prayer is a mighty, unifying activity and fosters shared love.

On Sunday, May 3, four days after the jury verdict, I drove with a friend to church. The streets were blessedly but eerily quiet. Along the way, we saw boarded up businesses, some spray-painted with the words "Black Owned," and a few people, brooms in hand, sweeping up the sidewalks and gutters. A pile of debris still smoldered at the corner where I turned to get to the church, and for a second, that queasiness returned and I wondered, "What will it look like?"

It was the last time I felt any vulnerability or anxiety. The church building was tall, untouched and serene. And inside, oh, my, what a joyful sound! And how much more deeply did I appreciate being able to share it! The singing was especially boisterous that morning, defiant, really, and the fellowship was jubilant. That reunion with my choir ever-strengthened our relationship, enabling a bond to grow that has never been broken.

But about two weeks after the violence had started in L.A., there was an incident at our church. The pastor, Fr. Patrick Walsh, was beginning the Liturgy of the Eucharist when suddenly, a stranger strode down the center aisle, all the way up to the altar. He had a megaphone and began to berate the congregation for having our church presided over by a white priest. (He did not mention me, although I was very obvious, in my place with the choir). I was not sure what would happen, but somehow, I felt no anxiety. Fr. Walsh seemed speechless, but he, too, did not look worried.

As the man continued his tirade, I felt a strong presence rise up in the church, a wave of strength and absolute determination. I looked around, and every man in the congregation was standing. These Christian men moved as if they were one, facing the man on the altar. They surrounded him, picked him up by the elbows, and carried him out of church—with him still shouting all along the way.

When the door closed behind the man who had been carried out, we heard someone clearly say, "You can go on, now, Father."

And Mass continued as if nothing had happened.

Throughout those days and weeks, I felt fear, dread, vulnerability, and great sadness. When civil upheavals occur, when the fabric of society tears to the point that violence is nearby or even at home, we are deeply, emotionally impacted. But in the midst of the fire, it is important to do all we can to take care, follow the instructions and orders given by those in authority, and not put ourselves in harm's way. It's also important to keep communication open, to take as much of the what-if worry about loved ones or community so that true and healing help can flourish.

Above all, what I learned from my experience is that church is powerful, especially against the negativity and breakdown that can occur in situations such as what happened in the spring of 1992 in Los Angeles. By "church," I don't mean only the building and the services and rituals that happen inside of it. I mean the community it creates, the fellowship, the ties, and how these become strong through a desired common purpose—the pursuit of spiritual grace, the better understanding of something beyond any human being and the reaching for God.

If we take God out of the equation to heal wounds caused by violence, we're left with only human solutions, which by their nature are imperfect.

But as we develop spiritual depth and understand evermore deeply how infinite the soul is in its capacity to take us beyond ourselves, our egos, and our human limitations, we find that God dwelling within brings us to wholeness. The whisper of grace inside moves us beyond misgivings or societally-manufactured hatred. And the common experience shared by people of faith in a time of trial binds all together beyond geography, ethnicity, or social status. Through my experience of refinement in the fire of the Los Angeles riots, I learned that God doesn't see color, and we don't, either, when we strive to see God.

With the riots over, my life continued. But as I've mentioned, it did not continue smoothly. Two years later, the world shook again—really: The Northridge earthquake was a wake-up call I'll never forget!

Living on Ground Not Our Own

In the wee hours of January 17, 1994, a chorus of car alarms and barking dogs broke into my sleep. A few seconds later came a low rumbling that grew louder as everything around me, including my bed, began to shake violently.

The shaking was caused by a magnitude 6.7 earthquake that had its epicenter in Northridge, California, about seventeen miles away. But the only thing I knew at that moment, was that my apartment and everything in it was spasming uncontrollably.

I leapt out of bed, shoved my feet into my firm-soled slippers (at the ready always), groped around for my eyeglasses, which had catapulted off my nightstand and landed on the floor a few feet away, and made for a reinforced doorway between my front hall and bathroom, staggering along as if I were trying to cross a roiling river on a flimsy suspension bridge. As I gripped the door jamb, the sound of falling books, papers, pictures, and vases came from the living room. The doors to the cupboards immediately to my right slammed open, and the contents inside flew past my head and landed on the floor around my feet.

As my hands dug into the door jamb, I remember thinking, "It has to stop sometime. It has to stop now. Stop now!" I also, fleetingly, wondered if the building would fall down completely.

Finally, the floor stopped shimmying beneath me and I could let go of the doorframe. I felt both spent and energized, dazed by the shock and grateful that I and the roof over my head were intact.

Then I heard loud banging at my front door. That startled me almost more than the quake had, but the sound focused my thoughts away from my own feelings and out to the world beyond my apartment. I opened my door and saw my two neighbors, students from Japan, trembling as they held onto each other. In halting English they asked me what was going on and did I have a flashlight or candles they could have, because the power was out.

I gave them what I could, and then we walked downstairs to the street, where many others had gathered in a shadowy, shell-shocked and wandering kind of block party. None of us knew the extent of the quake, damage, or even the details about magnitude or type (shallow, deep, which fault). As it was not even light, there wasn't much we could do except ensure that there had been no apartment collapses on our block, and everyone seemed unhurt.

Shortly after the first shaking, aftershocks followed, some almost as strong as the first temblor. I went back upstairs to my apartment to survey the damage, but I knew that, as long as the aftershocks were strong, there was no point in setting everything back in place.

As with the tornado I had lived through as a child, the damage within my apartment seemed oddly random. My living room and writing space were a mess, but nothing had fallen out of the kitchen cupboards so I, unlike many others, had no broken glass to deal with. I took stock of my food and water (which was also out, but I had bottled water on hand), grabbed my battery-operated radio, and settled in for what turned out to be several days of enduring many, many aftershocks and learning the true and devastating extent of what we now call the Northridge earthquake.

FAITH IN FOCUS

When we do not take even basic steps to prepare for emergencies, especially natural disasters, we might be setting ourselves up to fail. But when we gather some supplies and make other preparations, we create an atmosphere of proactive protection that can feed us with confidence. Make a preparedness list, and look into what is appropriate for where you live and what you might need. Reserve time to act on that list. Have faith that, as you prepare well, you will reap the soul-strengthening benefits even before a disaster might occur.

There were many things I learned from my experience then, and these have given me some insight into the importance of preparation before a crisis and gentleness during.

• Keep essential emergency supplies handy, even if you have never lived through a natural disaster or believe that one will never happen to you. During a crisis, you might not be able to locate what you need quickly or find someone who can give you what you need. Also, keep some extras on hand, just in case someone else needs your help.

• Trust your inner voice and react safely to a crisis. Know your escape routes, building safety zones, and how to contact loved ones in an emergency, keeping in mind that our usual areas or methods of communication might not be accessible or functional during or just after a disaster. If you have a pet, particularly a cat or a dog, do not discount that it might be able to sense an event before it occurs; I'll never forget hearing those dogs and car alarms just prior to Northridge striking.

• Use your deep physical and spiritual breathing tools to help steady you and give you however brief moments when you can try to gather your thoughts, orient yourself to what needs to be done next, and lift up prayers.

• Rely on a credible news source for guidance on where and when it is safe to move about your area and other vital information. Almost immediately after the first shaking, there were rumors flying about what had happened elsewhere—roads crushed, buildings demolished, people killed. Some of these turned out to be true, but others were proven to be false. Having a good source of news will help you be safe and well-informed.

• Understand that the effects of a devastating disaster, even if you live through it unhurt, are usually more than superficial. In the first few days after a shattering event, you might feel as if you are fine and normal, but subtly, slowly, you might come to understand that the crisis you've lived through has long tentacles that have reached into your heart and tipped the balance of your spirit. Your faith might still be very strong, but you could feel as if your spirit has been injured. Seek medical or spiritual help if you need it—don't think you have to be the hero at the expense of your own physical or emotional stability. And remember, be gentle to yourself as much as you are to others.

Taking Good Care

A crisis, by its very nature, will not be a warm and fuzzy kind of experience. It will not wrap you in security and comfort, and it will not provide stability. Even the most resilient person may feel deep pain. We, too, might take on some of this negative and often impersonal characteristic as we work our way through the crisis. For example, as our world shakes and breaks around us, it might seem quite natural to be angry, either at the event itself, at ourselves or other people, or at God. But resting on and stoking up such anger can sap precious energy, make it more difficult to think or act clearly. Anger could inflict more harm than the crisis itself in the long term, especially if we turn in anger toward loved ones or neighbors who are also reeling from the disaster. Anger toward ourselves could diminish our courage and make us feel like helpless victims instead of people who have been hurt but who have useful tools that can help us cope and rebuild.

In the aftermath of Northridge, I locked my keys in my car twice, something I'd never done before. The first time, I was embarrassed. The second time, I felt irritation rise within me; *How*, I wondered, *could I be so stupid?*

Then, I realized that my life and the community where I live had just undergone a horrible upheaval that was going to take months, if not years, to recover from, especially as the earthquake occurred only a little more than two years prior. But whereas the Los Angeles Riots had been eventually contained and controlled by a multiorganizational response from law enforcement and community leaders, the earthquake was in all ways an act of God, its beginning unpredictable and its ongoing, rollercoaster nature utterly unmanageable.

I had gone through the first wave of the earthquake by myself and had coped well, but in the days after the initial shock, I was nervous and unsettled. Anger at myself would have only increased my nervousness.

So I started to handle my nervous moments more gently and learned to laugh at my mishaps which, I decided, were not failings, but manifestations of my vulnerable spirit's calling for something much needed: tenderness and patience.

As I became more compassionate toward myself, I was able to be more understanding toward others, too. Truly, the need to be kind during a crisis does not stop with how we treat our loved ones, or even strangers. It has to extend to ourselves; the Spirit within needs our support, too! And by taking time to be kind to ourselves and spiritually recover, we are both acting out of respect for our precious lives and helping ourselves be as strong as we can be for those who also need us.

I also learned that in a crisis basic assumptions and other aspects of communicating become skewed, especially if the conversation field is uneven because one person has experienced the disaster and the other person has not. This disconnect is much akin to the phenomenon of armchair quarterbacking—insisting that you, the observer, know better what someone in the field should be doing.

From the point of view of someone experiencing the crisis, worldview narrows to the immediate and gradually moves beyond. For example, with the first shock, I was very focused on my limited world—myself, my possessions, my apartment. When my neighbors banged on my front door, the sound literally jarred me out of myself and opened my world up just a little more, making me realize that there were others who had experienced what I did. This worldview widened again when we walked out into the street and met others, some who were total strangers, who had similar questions and fears. Throughout all of these interactions, the shared experience of the earthquake made an underlying, smooth bond, a kind of kinship that brought support and relief. (Others knew, in this case, exactly what I was feeling, even if we manifested our emotions in different ways.)

When I began to interact with the outside world, that is, those who had not felt the earthquake, communicating became more of a challenge. It was also numbingly fatiguing as I sought to make others understand something that, from their perspective, was difficult if not impossible to grasp in its full magnitude (please, no pun intended).

For example, the business I worked for was not far from where I lived, but there was another office in a neighboring county. I remember getting a phone call at home from one of the people in that office, asking me why no one was picking up the telephone in the Los Angeles office that morning. In my little corner of the world, everyone knew that there was no possibility of businesses opening the day of the quake, and there was even uncertainty about when they would be able to resume operation. But just one county away, the earth was solid and firm, and the day was progressing as it normally would. I was at a loss to say when the office would open or what damage there might have been to it. I also did not know whether the LA employees had sustained damage to their homes, nor when or if they would be able to get to work. Having just sustained a 6.7 magnitude earthquake and multiple severe aftershocks, I felt mighty inadequate faced with those questions and my lack of answers!

Communicating with loved ones at a distance or accepting their physical presence and help can also be a challenge. The loved one will undoubtedly want to know exactly what has happened and what he or she can do to help. He or she might offer solutions and other ideas about what we should do, say, or feel. Not having been at ground zero, our loved one's help may or may not be appropriate, but we probably do not want to reject it outright. What a balancing act this can become—and a stressful one, too, especially during an ongoing, life-changing crisis! Yet it can also be a time to build trust and benefit from a loved one's fresh and strong spirit and energy, as long as the intent for everyone is not to bring more stress, but to alleviate as much of it as possible.

Two days after the initial jolt of the Northridge quake, my mother was due to visit me. She'd made her plans weeks in advance, and did not want to change them, not even because of a major natural disaster! Ordinarily, such visits were lots of fun, and I'd made some special plans for this one. However, a social visit from my beloved mother was not even remotely on my "must-do" list immediately following the quake. Museums, theaters, even shopping malls were all closed, as were most restaurants. And of course, in the back of my mind was the question of whether a strong aftershock would topple more buildings and, perhaps, mean that I wouldn't even have a home to welcome my mother into!

You can imagine the conversation we had when Mom asked, "Do you think I should still come? I want to."

"Mom, I'd love to see you, but I have no idea what you'll be walking into. There's part of a major freeway down, businesses are shut, a lot of roads are buckled, and the electricity has been off and on…"

Back and forth we went, until the picture I painted for her of the reality of the moment sunk in. Still, she decided to come, arriving just when the business where I worked was reopening—and picking up many scattered pieces. In those chaotic days that followed, Mom was a trouper and her visit a blessing for me in terms of support. She became used to the aftershocks and the complete change of plans brought about by the earthquake. She helped me set my apartment back to rights— and again and again after those aftershocks. She was even with me the second time I locked my keys in my car in the church parking lot and encouraged me to be gentle with myself. But it sure wasn't the visit either of us had envisioned when she booked her tickets weeks prior!

Natural disasters have a way of making all involved put their individual and collective egos aside!

Other crises invite us to give out abundant doses of gentleness, well-placed humor, and proverbial soft hugs. The loss of a loved one, which can leave a gash in our hearts, certainly calls for understanding and kindness. Receiving a diagnosis of a life-threatening disease calls for an embrace of patient understanding and unconditional compassion—from those around us, and also from ourselves. A devastating blow of any kind might simply call for hot, salty tears—a cleansing cry—which is another very valid way to help ourselves gently shed sadness and begin to fill up with peace.

Sometimes, we might hesitate to minister to someone in a crisis, fearing we can't do much to help. However, we do not need to feel as if we have to move mountains—a simple, "Please let me know if there is anything I can do for you," is a blessed expression of care. Or suggesting ways to bring relief, however brief, to the burdens of someone dealing with a crisis, can be a strong demonstration of compassion. Offering to watch the children for an afternoon, run errands, or be a nonjudgmental shoulder to cry on are a few more ways to put gentleness into practice.

We might also not know how to accept being comforted, worried that, if we slouch instead of maintaining our posture of strength, we will somehow fall short or, worse, show weakness and thus fail. Many men might relate to this, because men are often expected to bear tremendous burdens of outward strength devoid of any show of sadness or other emotion.

Yet deep emotional breathing, expressing our feelings through tears, sighs, words, and gestures can not only be relieving, but can be a valuable tool to teach children and others about the overall journey we go through in a crisis—from difficulty and often sorrow, through a sometimes jagged rebuilding process, on to greater strength. We are more likely to help children learn the appropriate way to express themselves, helping grow an emotionally and spiritually healthful cycle of response to adversity. And by accepting comfort from others, we are also allowing them to carry out a blessed ministry—sharing love that, too, comes from God's wonderful Spirit!

Crisis Within

The Los Angeles Riots threatened the fabric of multicultural Los Angeles, the city where I lived. The Northridge earthquake threatened the foundations of homes throughout the southern California area, including mine. But the crisis that occurred and is still very real struck more than close to home—it altered my way of living forever and also threatened my life.

A few years after Northridge, I began to feel ill. My hair fell out in large clumps; my hands were weak and unsteady. I began to drop things unexpectedly and had difficulty even holding onto a toothbrush. Odd rashes appeared on my face and elsewhere. I was extremely tired and began to have spiking fevers, especially in the afternoons.

At first, my doctor told me I was stressed. But finally, nearly a year from when I felt ill, lab work, tests, and a thorough examination by a rheumatologist revealed that I had systemic lupus erythematosus, an autoimmune illness where the body produces antibodies to its own tissue and causes painful and sometimes destructive inflammation in organs such as the skin, kidneys, lungs, and central nervous system. The opposite of AIDS and cancer, in lupus, the immune system is overactive. There is no cure for lupus, and only one lupus-specific medication has been developed in the last fifty years to treat certain forms of the disease.

Each person who has lupus has a unique set of symptoms. In my case, lupus activity had progressed beyond mild, threatening my life and requiring my immediate attention. All of my hair fell out, and my face was obviously marked with the hallmark butterfly-like rash across my cheeks. My platelet count dropped, my heart valves were affected, I had permanently lost some of my hearing, and my joints were inflamed and painfully swollen.

Immediately, I had to quit my job and most of my other activities, change my diet, avoid sunlight, and start a regimen of very potent medications that had challenging side effects and no guarantee of efficacy. I assembled a medical team across multiple specialties, including a rheumatologist, cardiologist, and hematologist. My life revolved around doctors, symptom management, prayer, nonrestorative sleep, and immersing myself in the new language of lupus. I had no idea what lupus was when I was diagnosed, let alone how it was treated or what it would mean to my life. But I did know that I did not want to die and suspended my fear long enough to start fighting—and learning all I could about the disease that had become an ongoing presence in my life.[14]

I also learned who my true friends were and who in my social circle would not be supportive as I cancelled activities, some at the last minute, because of my profound fatigue and other symptoms. I lost several friends in those early days, which hurt me emotionally. But in retrospect, I understand that some people are not yet at the point where they have the patience and compassion necessary to have a relationship with someone who is chronically ill. And in their place, I have found remarkable people, some who are patients themselves, who have an abundance of empathy and love and who have become fast, true friends.

As lupus continued to flare, I developed extreme dizziness and a condition called Sjögren's syndrome, which causes extreme, external and internal dryness. I was constantly plagued with infections and began to think I was sending my pharmacist's three children through college! And throughout these early days, my doctors repeatedly urged me to avoid stress! (Those who treat and live with lupus, I've learned, must develop a good sense of humor.)

When life is interrupted by a crisis, especially one that pulls us from one direction and turns us toward a completely different one, we can feel a very deep and frightening sense of doubt. Health crises are perhaps the most difficult of all to endure because often they continue through long stretches of time—sometimes for years. They impact all aspects of life, from finances to work, from family to other relationships. They also inevitably direct us to consider our spirituality from the perspective of mortality and God's participation in our suffering and, perhaps, our desire to be cured, as well as our overall purpose and relationship to the world.

I asked myself (and God) a lot of questions in those early days: Was I who I thought I was? Had my purpose in life changed? If so, to what?

At that point in my journey, I didn't think, "What if...?" or even, "What is...?" because both were unknown territories for me. So often, I found myself just wondering, "What?" But not, "Why?" or, "Why me?"

I realize these are natural questions to ask, and I know many people with serious chronic illnesses who have wondered these more than once. However, for me, I found, and still find, the question is besides the point. I don't really ask, "Why me?" because, simply, it *is* me. No amount of wondering why I got lupus, lived through two tornadoes, civil unrest, a major earthquake, and more would change the reality that I had, I did, and I was still living.

Living Throughout

Just as I have told the many lupus patients and others whom I've met since my journey began, lupus—and all life's crises—just are. The point is what we do with them.

This is the bridge that takes me away from "Why?" and toward something actionable and tangible. By reasoning as I did, I was able to start to find the what-is moment that would turn the pain, broken relationships, altered lifestyle, and other trouble into gifts through which I could seek to be stronger in the Spirit and closer to God. And seek, I did.

I read the Bible more than ever before, praying over my life, faith, and God's presence. I wrote about my experiences, pain, the upheaval around and in me. The questions, "What is my purpose, now? What is my ministry?" permeated all of my meditation, and gradually I began to realize that God's will for me was not somewhere outside of my experience with lupus. It was integral to that experience.

I cannot lie and say that I have enjoyed much of the pain and upheaval of life with lupus. But I can say that not dwelling on a plaintive "Why me?" has aided me tremendously to move forward toward life-supporting things such as learning about the disease, and what I have to do to be as healthful as possible and then acting on that knowledge.

If we keep thinking we are victims, we will be less likely to take charge of our education, and thus, our actions as they relate to our diagnosis. But if we resolve to learn and work with our doctors on an action plan, we will feel more control, less stress, and thus, be less likely to panic.

Loss is a huge component of any serious diagnosis. But if we replace the loss with something positive, we can help ourselves accept and find more good in the new than in the old. One example in my own life: I cannot change the fact that I don't have my thick, naturally blond hair anymore. But I can choose a variety of wigs and never have a bad hair day!

Expanding my focus beyond "Why me?" to others around me helped me understand their responses to my illness, learn to cultivate true friends and make new ones, and let go of relationships that were not helpful but, quite the contrary, were toxic to my spiritual and physical well-being.

Allowing my conversations with God to move past asking him, "Why?" has also helped me to discern the purpose of this new life. I feel as if I'm more of an adult, seeking guidance and open to growing further, instead of being a child who repeats the same question over and over, "Why? Why?" without realizing there is a rich world beyond.

I was diagnosed with lupus nearly eighteen years ago. Since then, the twists and turns of the disease, at times quiet, at times fully aflare, have sometimes felt like the Los Angeles Riots or Northridge earthquake have taken up residence inside of me. But throughout, the unexpected abundance of life never ceases to amaze me. I have met people I never would have otherwise, wonderful, strong, courageous people with stories of crisis and survival that make for great inspiration and encouragement. Through my need to take great care of health, I have learned how amazing and wonderful our bodies are, and how vulnerable and precious this life is.

Lupus has made me much more proactive about advocating for myself and others. It has taught me to not be afraid of questioning doctors, speaking with specialists, and navigating the maze of red tape that is modern health care. Deep down, living with a chronic illness has also given me great confidence that God is ever-present and ready to comfort and guide. The times when I've felt most at a crossroads, I've heard that soft voice within prompt me to take the best course. And the times I've been most down, or even felt distanced from an immediate sense of spiritual strength, all I've had to do is pray, and the distance falls away, and in its place is tremendous comfort within and all around.

CHAPTER SIX
Singed but Safe

I have many Bibles on my bookshelves and nightstand. But one that holds great meaning for me is an old copy of the Jerusalem Bible, which my mother gave to her parents many years ago. A few years after she gave it to them, there was a fire in the living room of my grandparents' house. Most of the objects, including the carpeting and furniture, were damaged beyond salvaging—but not this Bible. Besides the slightly browned underside of the pages, it is intact; not a bit of the fire or smoke marred any of the pages inside, where the heart of the book resides.

After my grandfather died, my grandmother gave the Bible back to my mother and she then passed it along to me. Its meaning for me is one of beautiful survival despite damage, survival and endurance of the spirit. Singed but safe.

This is particularly powerful for me now, given all of the crises I've lived through since receiving it. As we go through the fire of a crisis, we feel pain in many ways. Fear, too, and loss that might linger sadly with us for a long time. But although we might be quite singed from a crisis, the Spirit within dwells far beyond any lasting human pain or loss. With good care of that essence of who we are, that Spirit, we are safe. Moreover, we are able to put fear in its place—outside of ourselves—and benefit from calm and peace in moments that are frightfully beyond our control.

What Do You Do with Fear?

In the middle of the fire, in the midst of a crisis, it is natural to feel fear, to have moments of nervous hesitation, trembling, shaking, or shock. Fear can propel us into nearly rabid what-ifs? For example, we might wonder if we will survive the ordeal or if we will live but be faced with horrible devastation in the aftermath.

Through cultivation of the Spirit—those spiritual deep breaths, prayer, reflection, and other inner practices, as well as outward actions such as worship or acts of charity—you can establish a vibrant connection between your world and the good that is inside of you and beyond you. You forge a relationship with God.

As we build a stronger connection to that Spirit within us, acknowledging that we are more than a physical body or emotional response in life, we find that what we thought were our limits are, actually, no limits at all. What we thought was fear is actually the ability to have courage.

Perhaps we feared we would be incapable of withstanding days without restorative sleep because we needed to sit by a loved one's hospital bedside. But through dedication (digging deep within to express our love) and patience (a virtue that springs from a willing and loyal spirit), we persevered—with less exhaustion than we'd imagined. Perhaps we saw a news story about a natural disaster in a distant land and thought, "I would absolutely fall apart if that happened to me." Yet, when devastation occurred, we were emotionally shaken but spiritually carried along by inner grace, support that we sense comes from God. We moved beyond our fears, we persevered.

Or perhaps we found ourselves in a situation we did not expect at all, suddenly, violently. A fearful situation that threatened our life. Yet, we who have been diligent about building spiritual strength discovered that, even when our hearts were frozen with fear and our physical capabilities were literally tied up, the Spirit was unfettered. It acts when we cannot, and it sets us free.

Deacon Michael Bellinder found himself in such a situation, and far from becoming consumed with the fire-filled crisis that beset him, he reached inside, to the Spirit, and was able to find grace.

I first met Michael when he and I were asked to appear as guests on the television program, *The Word in the World*. We were on different episodes, so I sat in the studio audience while Michael related his amazing story. When I was trying to think of people who have relied on spirituality to navigate a life-threatening crisis, I immediately contacted him about going into more detail about his ordeal and its aftermath so that readers of this book might be inspired by his story, too.

A family man and devout Catholic, Michael was committed to his community, church, and work. One evening, he and a coworker were securing the door to the cable company where they worked when five men in ski masks forced their way in.

"One of them grabbed my throat," Michael recounts. "I was looking down at the barrel of a gun. He squeezed my throat very hard. I thought, *Lord, tell me what to say.*"

The words that sprang out of Michael's mouth resonated with his entire life of commitment to family. "I said, 'Please don't shoot me. I have a wife and kids at home.'"

The intruder swore at him, then ordered Michael and his colleague to kneel on the floor with their noses to the ground. Then the man began to quiz Michael about the cars in the parking lot.

"He said, 'Why are there three cars in the lot and only two of you coming out? Who drove the third car?' I told him, 'I drive the Volvo,' and he kicked me in the face and pistol-whipped me. Then, he said, 'If there's anyone else in the building, you're a dead man. I'm going to kill you.'"

Was Michael afraid? There didn't seem to be much time to register fear. The intruders duct-taped Michael's and his coworker's hands behind their backs, and taped their eyes, too. "I didn't know who belonged to the third car," Michael says. "I didn't know who else was in the building."

But at any moment, if someone else appeared, he knew what the consequences would be.

Beaten, bound, and knowing that the very worst could happen, Michael could have understandably been paralyzed with fear. But even in cases such as these, when our emotions are stifled and we are physically restricted, the Spirit is working.

"I went into prayer at that moment," Michael told me. Michael's early education was in Catholic schools. There, he learned many prayers, including the Act of Contrition, a prayer that asks for God's forgiveness, a cleansing of past sins. The prayer is part of the sacrament of the sick, often administered when a person is dying.

"I remember the nuns always said, 'When you're near death, pray the Act of Contrition.'"

So he started to pray, "Oh, my God, I am heartily sorry for having offended Thee, and I confess to Thee all my sins for Thy just punishment, but most of all because they offend Thee, my God, who art all good and deserving of all my love. I firmly resolve with the help of Thy grace to sin no more, and to avoid the near occasion of sin."

Michael told me, "I prayed it silently, but as it progressed, it got louder and louder, and I prayed it aloud. They weren't going to stop me from praying."

Suddenly, Michael felt very different, supported and protected. "This overwhelming sense of peace began to overtake my entire being. I felt like I was lifted by ten thousand angels."

The two men returned just then. They had not found anyone else in the building. (Michael later learned that the third car had run out of gas, and the employee to whom it belonged had left work in another car.) They wanted to steal cable boxes from the warehouse, so they asked if there were any alarms that needed to be turned off. Then, they led Michael and his colleague to another area, separated them, and left them there.

"When they broke into the warehouse, I still had an incredible sense of peace," Michael told me. "I heard my colleague escape across the hall, and then the sound of what I thought was a truck backing up." If it had been, the ordeal would have been nearing an end.

Tragically, it wasn't.

Unbeknownst to Michael, there was an active alarm in the warehouse, and when the intruders broke in, it went off.

"It was a loud alarm," Michael said. "I heard the patter of feet, a lot of commotion, and a blast that shook the room. Then, I felt a warm sensation in my back, and I went down to the ground."

He was seriously wounded, although he did not know then to what extent. Still bound and gagged, he lay on the ground and formed three words that managed to flow from his mouth, unexpected but clear.

"I said, 'I forgive you.' It was a gift from the Holy Spirit. I believe it was God reaching out to the man who shot me."

It was also a turning point in Michael's life, although he did not realize it just then. Rather, as happens in many crises, there was a very long way to travel before he could discern the purpose of his ordeal, especially that moment of forgiveness, and be able to act on it.

No End in Sight?

It would be easier for us if every crisis were one, single episode and nothing more. This would give us ample time to think about what has happened and assimilate the lessons learned and tangible consequences.

But as we all know and the oft-repeated adage goes, "When it rains, it pours."

Sometimes, crises come rapidly, one after the other, and involve more than just the original, precipitating event. The Los Angeles Riots, for example, resulted in business and personal losses that I'm sure took months, if not years, for those affected to deal with. The Northridge earthquake also caused a cascade of problems large and small for people who lost buildings or loved ones, and the city and other officials certainly had to manage all sorts of infrastructure problems as the damage was assessed and cleaned up.

In a health crisis such as the one I experienced, the initial shock of a life-threatening illness brought up many other issues, large and small, that required my attention at a time when my nerves were worn thin with, well, issues. Insurance matters, finding the right doctors, even understanding a whole new language—medicalese—so that I could take an active part in my care, these took time and energy in short supply. But they had to be dealt with—although sometimes it's like trying to stop up holes in a dam with only my fingers…and sometimes, you just run out of fingers!

It is one thing to be a first responder or someone who travels to places devastated by natural disasters and witnesses suffering, perhaps taking that suffering on yourself. But to be an ordinary person just doing your job—I mean, who among us expects to be involved in an armed robbery and assault in the workplace, let alone deal with the time and issues afterward, including police questioning, surgery, medication, and acute, ongoing pain?

For Michael, the aftermath of his ordeal was focused on things he probably never imagined he'd have to deal with. The bullet that had gone into the side of his spine could be extracted, but even today, he continues to have foot, toe, and back problems. The ordeal took a toll that led to a very difficult two-year period when he struggled to cope with his physical and emotional trauma. He even stepped away from his diaconate.

But, most importantly, he did not step away from life.

In the darkest times, we might fear there is no way back to physical, emotional, and spiritual health. Even if the roads around us—work, life as we'd known it, health, and regular practice of faith—seem blocked, within us is a deep, present, and abiding Spirit that holds keys to newness for us always. The important thing is that we do not fear to continue and that we do not give up. We must walk through the hard times in order to reach better ones, and we often undergo refinement, much like gold does when it is heated and reshaped into something beautiful, so that we can reemerge in bright newness. This is especially how I viewed my diagnosis of lupus; it was going to require all of my strength and inner resources as it changed my life, removing many of the things that I had previously enjoyed (health, hair, friends, and daytime tennis matches, for example). But I had faith that I could turn to spiritual practices, loved ones, and other long-nurtured supports and, eventually, reemerge.

Whether I am in the midst of picking up the pieces from a crisis, or I think that the initial shock is past but more trouble might be brewing, here are some of the things I do to allow my body, mind, and spirit to be protected and comforted:

• If I'm constantly looking back over my shoulder to see if another trouble is following me, I'll undoubtedly trip! If I think I have to tackle a crisis or other huge problem all at once, I'll crumple under unreasonable pressure. So I try to keep my focus on the necessary moment of the day. Take care of the problems at hand first, and if you find yourself completely overwhelmed, break down your activity into smaller segments. Everything will be handled in good time.

• I surround myself with love, kindness, good humor, and relaxation. If I need to cry, I allow myself that blessed luxury, too. I tend to my hurts, my pain as gently and lovingly as I would do for someone else. I follow my doctor's orders, if appropriate. I consider rest and other beneficial activities as part of my treatment and part of the road to recovery. I take small steps each day toward healing—breathing in and out in healthy ways.

• I am aware of my vulnerability. I know that the time during and after a trauma is probably not good for making important, life-altering decisions or opening myself up to anything that might be risky or overly challenging. When I am stronger and my heart is healed, I might reconsider these things—or, more likely, I might discover that I have grown so beyond them that they are no longer needed or important.

• I will be singed during any crisis. And if other trouble ensues from the original problem, I might be singed badly. It's very helpful to be realistic about what the situation *is*, and not what we *fear* it is or will become. A crisis (or two or three) is trouble enough—there's no help or healing in forever worrying about more!

• I am mindful of the place for prayer. I pray all through my day, especially if I'm in a crisis. This benefits my spirit, nerves, heart, and head. When we're consumed by a crisis or resulting hurt, often we push out prayer and thoughts of the Spirit because negative influences around us (and within, as they are from pain) are so overwhelming. By consciously keeping a place within me and beside me for prayer, I'll be able to nurture strength within for even the toughest of times.

Michael's foundation of faith and the deep spirituality he'd cultivated throughout his life provided him with support, too. He also had true friends—loved ones—especially at home.

"My wife is a strong person," he says, "She told me, 'You're not going to get rid of me.'"

Additional support from doctors and others helped, too. But perhaps most importantly, Michael allowed himself to move through the aftermath. Some people might have been unwilling to take the first step toward healing, but Michael persisted, opting for the road to recovery that required great trust and patience.

We live in such an instant world, where results are expected to be quick and lives are expected to move ahead, that we forget about the importance and the power of time. It is impossible to make complete sense of a crisis unless we allow enough time to pass (and work on clarity during that time) to work through any physical residue, emotional issues, and most especially, spiritual aspects of what we've been through. As much as we'd like others to carry our burdens for us, and to resolve any loose ends, the aftermath is ours to work through, understand, and benefit from. Only then do we receive the full blessing of what the crisis teaches and the transformation it can make.

Bolstered by his early spiritual and faith practices and evidenced by the fact that, even at the darkest time, he still had faith, Michael did not give up. With positive influences and abiding grace, gradually he could reconnect with his Spirit and nurture that light to burn brightly again.

"I totally turned my life around when I made a commitment to Christ over a Cursillo weekend," he told me, "and I also did an Immaculate Heart of Mary dedication."[15]

Renewed, Michael serves as a deacon in a Catholic church in Southern California. He also frequently gives talks, especially to young people, and shares his love of the simple prayer that started his ability to heal: the Act of Contrition. "I hand out small copies of it," he says to me, now. "I look back now, at that two-year period as a purification process. The Lord is using me in so many more ways than he ever did before."

There is wonder in Michael's voice at the way the road to healing happened, and an eagerness to continue to tell his story so others may be helped and healed. Most importantly, there is no bitterness or anger, no hatred and no hint of carrying a grudge.

"The forgiveness experience allowed me not to carry baggage of hatred and revenge with me," he says. "In fact, saying, 'I forgive you,' may have saved my life."

Leaving Our Burdens Behind

In an age when long-held grudges play out in wars, terrorist attacks, riots, and one-on-one hostilities, pure, true, complete forgiveness might seem to be in short supply. Yet, when we have witnessed its power in our lives or in situations that play across the world stage, we see that when people can forgive wrongs, no matter how deep and awful they are, peace and good flood the souls of all involved. Forgiveness can build back lives that would otherwise have been lost, as Michael Bellinder recognized; by being able to truly forgive, he was not held hostage by his pain and overturned life. He could move ahead with positive dedication, ahead in goodness, and reach out to others who are also hurting.

Forgiveness can allow us to make good out of a less-than-ideal situation, even years after a terrible pain is first inflicted on us.

As a child, we moved around a lot, and as I grew older, each move became more difficult. One time, we were living in a community I really liked and thrived in. In less than a year, I made good friends, discovered a love for the theatrical stage, starred in our school play (*Camelot*—I played Guinevere!), and felt endless possibilities for the next school year. But just as I was enjoying a happy time, my parents told me and my brother that we were going to have to move again, and this time to another state.

I was devastated. I got very angry, and my anger demonstrated itself in how I started interacting with the children at my new school. Nothing about the new community, school, or classes could live up to what I had enjoyed before and lost! Not a good way to make new friends or get settled in. What an angry time that was, and how that anger heightened my unhappiness!

Gradually, I was able to find activities that eased me into meeting new friends; music, theater, writing—I discovered I could do them in my new home, too. I realized I couldn't do anything about moving to a better environment, old or new, until I could leave for college, and that realization—recognizing what is and letting go of the what-ifs helped, too.

The singed feeling I had from moving so much as a child left some scars—it still takes me awhile to adjust to major life changes, and I still do not like even the thought of moving house and home. But as I understand how freeing it is to let go of the burden of anger and the feeling of being wronged, I find I desire that positive feeling more than holding onto hatred, and blessedly, forgiveness comes much more easily than it otherwise would. Truly, forgiveness can enable us to be more positive about any trouble that happens to us; it can be one less negative element dragging down our Spirit and our ability to cope. It can enable us to be less prone to panic!

Aside from my own experiences with forgiveness, I have a personal connection with a very public one that has also been influential for me.

On Sunday, October 7, 1979, I was honored to be part of the choir that sang for the papal Mass on the Mall in Washington, DC. It was only one year before that Pope John Paul II had been elected, and the U.S. visit, culminating with an open-air Mass, was tremendously exciting, especially for those of us closely involved in part of it.

The choir was positioned behind and to the right of the altar area, and we had a perfect, close view of the Holy Father as he processed in. What struck me most was the way he waved, arm not only raised, but moving high and around, as if by his gesture he was including everyone and everything in a gesture of joy. That joy was also in his face—smiling not just with the mouth, but with the eyes. And it was contagious—you could not help but put extra energy into music or prayer with that kind of expressed love.

Camera bug that I am, I couldn't resist raising my hand and snapping pictures even as we were singing! My lens captured the pope's smiling entrance—a keeper that I have tucked in one of my favorite photo albums.

The memories and spirit of participating in the papal Mass were still resonating strongly with me when, in 1981, Pope John Paul II was shot by a man who professed hatred for him. The video and still pictures shocked people throughout the world; there was something especially horrific about the crimson stain of blood on bright white papal vestments. I couldn't help but think of the picture I still had of the exuberant, loving man joyfully greeting throngs of people on the Washington Mall. I wondered how anyone could have so much hatred that they were not swept up in, or at least subdued by, the good Spirit of the man who was serving his flock in stellar faith.

FAITH IN FOCUS

Is there anyone in your life against whom you hold a grudge? How is it affecting your peace of soul and mind, or what you do and say? Consider ways you might forgive the one who has wronged you and put your anger and agitation to rest. Act positively to invite healing. Have faith that you are not being weak, but rather are ridding yourself of a burden that is holding you back from making the most and best out of the rest of your life.

_____

_____

_____

_____

_____

_____

Throughout the world, prayers flowed for healing for the Pope and the two others in the crowd who were also shot by the gunman. I wonder how many people also prayed for the shooter, Mehmet Ali Agca? I cannot remember doing so, but I also cannot remember feeling hatred toward him; my thoughts at the time were really focused on the victims. But I did still wonder, "Why?"

As the days and months moved on, the story of the shooting and subsequent trial and conviction of Agca gradually moved from the front page to inside page of most newspapers, and finally, it became no more than a passing remark. Then, two years after the attack, another story came forward, unexpected, surprising, and freshly faith-filled. Pope John Paul II, who had endured the pain of being shot, the sharp sting of someone's hatred, and also the pain of knowing that two other innocent people had been harmed during the same incident, paid a personal visit to the man who had caused such pain.

During that visit, he forgave Mehmet Ali Agca.

I remember the excited buzz about their meeting, how people reacted to it with shock, then delight, or disbelief, and then amazement. It had much of the same feel as the brilliantly sunny day a few years earlier at the Mass on the Mall in Washington—a sense of freedom, release, and renewal. I realized then, as I have each time I have experienced the wonder and cleansing of forgiveness or seen it occur in others, that the more we open ourselves to moving beyond personal hurt to healing, we become stronger and more whole, we become more effective people, and we are able to move ahead harboring promise and hope, leaving behind anger that would otherwise keep us bound up.

Taking Time to Heal

Forgiveness and healing are processes, not things that can happen overnight. Moreover, there is no one, correct time frame for forgiveness. It is, like so much else, an individual thing, and cannot be forced, and it is not complete without two important components: internal cleansing and external expression.

FAITH IN FOCUS

Take time to explore examples of forgiveness that you have witnessed or have experienced in your life. What were the emotions you felt? What were the tangible acts that carried that forgiveness into individuals and communities? What were the fruits of that forgiveness? Have faith that, the more you recognize the beauty of forgiveness, the more its peace will rest in your life—and the less likely you will be to panic when any trouble arises.

_____

_____

_____

_____

_____

_____

In the midst of his crisis, Michael Bellinder uttered the words, "I forgive you," as he lay on the floor, bound and shot. But in the long months that followed, those words had to take root as he worked through rehab and put his life back together so that he could reach a point where his words met his Spirit and lifted him up.

Two years after the attack on him and two others, Pope St. John Paul II visited his attacker in prison and forgave him. It was two years during which the Pope healed, and the justice system worked on trying Agca—two very distinct processes that had to run their full course before the meeting, and forgiveness, could occur.

I couldn't shake my anger and disappointment from having to move away from friends as a child, but I gradually shed that burden as I matured, grew closer to God, and realized that grudges only hurt; they don't help. Sometimes, we might be able to say, "It's OK," or "I forgive you," and move ahead without any negative consequences. Sometimes, though, we might have to go through a more extended and painful process of healing, often sliding back into anger and bitterness before we can reach peace.

Here are some things that I've found helpful in our efforts to find a way to forgive:

- Do the necessary things to heal physically, emotionally, and spiritually. Consult your physician, counselor, clergyperson, and other trusted individuals in order to support your efforts in healing.
- Focus on bringing light to your soul—refuse to let the darkness of anger occupy your prayers or expressions of faith. Engage in good, nurturing activities that further strengthen your ability to listen to the Spirit within you.
- Consider the value of all life and extend that consideration to the life of the person who wronged you. In this way, you can begin to separate your anger at the offending act from understanding that the other person, however wrong, is a human being, just as you are.
- Imagine yourself forgiving the person who wronged you. Replay your meeting and, if possible, find an opportunity to face the other person with your forgiveness.
- Speak the words, "I forgive you." Let them carry out any vestige of resentment. Allow your spirit to move ahead in hope. As long as we carry past hurts with us and allow them to rub and rub at the wounds they have caused, we will still feel pain from them. That pain will, in turn, make it more difficult for us to face potential or real future crises with pure strength and courage because knowing how awful past hurts did and still torment us, we will dread facing any fresh ones. Still horribly singed, we won't feel secure; we won't feel safe.

But when we are able to get past those deep hurts, whether inflicted by strangers or loved ones, we can fill ourselves with more positive energy, resolve, wisdom, and strength. We can be assured that our lives ahead need not be overwhelmed by residual suffering. And we can know that, no matter how difficult our next crisis can be, we will be able to bounce back.

Like the precious, browned Jerusalem Bible that now sits on a shelf within view of where I am now writing, the fire of a crisis can leave us singed, making the aftermath a tremendous challenge. But if we are determined to see it through, to rebuild in a positive way that cleanses us from burdens of resentment and anger, we will be safe from bitterness and will be free to be of new and good use in the days and years to come.

CHAPTER SEVEN

The Power and Presence of Prayer

Talking to God: This is my definition of prayer.

And although that might sound like a simplistic definition, it is not meant to be. Prayer is a complex activity that engages all of our senses and sensibility. At every age and stage of life, prayer can be spiritually transformative and emotionally moving. It can enable us to find wisdom and courage, and it can also help us accept that which cannot be changed, however we might pray it would be. In the midst of a crisis, it can help us breathe in peace and exhale resolve, and through prayer, we can find clarity of heart and mind to jump into action for ourselves or others.

But for all of the intricacy involved in prayer, and the different and sometimes divergent opinions about it, I still think that the time we spend in prayer is spent talking to God, communicating with the Creator.

When I pray, I know that I am not talking to myself!

Science and Spirit

I pray more than once every day, and I am not alone. For 55 percent of Americans surveyed by the Pew Research Center in 2013, prayer is a daily activity, and even 21 percent of those surveyed who said they were not affiliated with a religion said they pray daily.[16]

For those who pray daily and consider it a cornerstone of their spirituality, prayer is a vital support throughout all of life, whether in a crisis or not. For those who have not yet ventured into prayer, there are even scientific reasons to at least explore it.

One of the biggest misunderstandings about prayer is that it is an activity that has no tangible effect or result. I've heard some people say that prayer is a superstitious reflex with no basis in reality. I've known a few people who will even go so far as to say it is a waste of time, that because they do not believe in God, there is no point acknowledging that prayer has value. But it's hard to imagine that so many people do something regularly that has no effect at all! And when we look at some of the scientific response to the subject of prayer, we begin to find reasons why prayer is so integral to many people's lives.

According to the National Center for Complementary and Integrative Health, prayer is considered to be a complementary and alternative (CAM) health practice. In a 2004 survey, prayer was one of the ten most commonly used CAM practices (others among the top ten included yoga, meditation, natural products, and deep breathing exercises),[17] and the forms of prayer listed were praying for one's own health condition, for someone else's health condition, and participating in a group prayer activity.

Because so many people rely on prayer as part of their spiritual and physical lives, scientists have begun to take a closer look at what, if any, health effect prayer has. Designing prayer studies is difficult because there are so many ways people pray, and it is such a highly personal and, often, silent activity. Even so, some respected scientists have found intriguing results from some studies.

Neurologist Andrew Newberg, MD, and colleagues have used modern imaging technology (fMRI) to note changes in brain activity in people who practice prayer, discovering that certain areas of the brain associated with better outlook and coping are positively affected by deep prayer and other religious activity.[18] Data from another study, conducted in England in 2008, that also used fMRI technology, suggest that religious experience, including prayer, lessened the perception of pain felt by study participants who voluntarily submitted themselves to electrical shock.[19]

A 2012 study conducted at the Royal Adelaide Hospital Cancer Centre in South Australia found "small but significant improvements in spiritual well-being" in patients who received intercessory prayer (that is, for whom others prayed).[20] And a meta-analysis that reviewed the published studies on personal prayer and patients living with chronic illness concluded that, although the body of literature to date (2015) has significant limitations and inadequacies, personal prayer can be "regarded as a strategy to cope and to connect with a higher source, providing meaning and hope."[21]

More studies will undoubtedly be forthcoming. For example, the Institute for Spirituality and Health at the Texas Medical Center and Baylor College of Medicine are planning a study to use fMRI technology to look at the effects of spirituality, especially prayer, on the brain.[22] But as I have experienced in my own life and witnessed in others' lives, we do not have to wait for science to catch up with what we already know: Prayer is one of the most powerful spiritual activities we can engage in, and that power, when nurtured and grown, can provide immense support for us in very trying times.

Although some people use prayer as a way to lift up a list of petitions to God, I do not. For me, prayer is powerful, not because I use it to get things I want or because I feel some kind of supernatural stirring during prayer. No, prayer is a way for me to connect with God and find strength, comfort, and courage no matter what health situation or other crisis I might face. I pray in good times, too, and very often my prayer is simply, "Thank you, God!" a kind of hallelujah full of thanks and joy. I pray for others, especially that they, too, will have strength abundant to face their own trials. And in a crisis, prayer is a fundamental activity through which I strive to find wisdom and comfort.

Getting Started or Continuing On Your Way

Someone once told me that if you look at a tree and say, "What a beautiful tree!" you are praying—expressing appreciation and gratitude for something God, not you, made. In that way, I think each of us prays more than we realize—and those who feel they do not pray are probably doing it anyway!

Prayer need not be something we turn into only a prescribed ritual, but can take many forms, both pre-established and improvised. However it is practiced, of course, as with any healthful habit, the more attention we pay to it, the more we benefit from it.

Anyone at any time can learn to pray, be more conscious of praying, or deepen his or her existing prayer life. I happened to begin at a young age, when it always seemed I was getting ill. Not just childhood illnesses, but long bouts of pneumonia and other awful and, a few times, odd sicknesses. During those weeks when I'd be in bed at home, isolated from friends and even family, my mother told me, "If you are physically alone, you can always talk to God."

I cannot express fully how deeply those words ignited a curiosity and longing in me that continues to this day! Talk to God? Amazing!

As I was young, then, I first learned traditional prayers handed down by generations and generations of Catholics.

Angel of God, my guardian dear, to whom His love commits me here, ever this day be at my side to light to guard to rule and guide.

And, *Our Father, Who art in heaven, hallowed be Thy name. Thy kingdom come, Thy will be done on earth as it is in heaven. Give us this day our daily bread and forgive us our trespasses as we forgive those who trespass against us. And lead us not into temptation, but deliver us from evil.*

And, *Hail Mary, full of grace, the Lord is with thee. Blessed art thou among women and blessed is the fruit of thy womb, Jesus. Holy Mary, Mother of God, pray for us sinners now and at the hour of our death. Amen.*

These memorized prayers were comforting because of their words and also because of their cadence and language. There was something fascinating about the world of these prayers that made me want to learn more—angels and grace, life and death. And they certainly were more compelling than *Dick and Jane* and other homework reading I had to do!

FAITH IN FOCUS

How do you talk to God? Do you address God in any particular way? Where is God when you pray? Consider the specifics of your prayer life and become more aware of the presence of the one to whom you pray each time you begin. Have faith that, as you develop a greater awareness of your prayer life, you will deepen your understanding of the Spirit, and your conversations with God will take on greater depth, too.

_____

_____

_____

_____

_____

_____

About this time, I sensed there was more to the world of praying than repeating memorized words. Not that there was anything wrong with them; I love these prayers and still pray these and others daily.

Memorized prayers can assist in gaining focus in a fuzzy world, and they can also help us articulate what we sometimes are unable to say. But when we talk to someone, even God, we speak as ourselves, however inarticulate we might fear we are! So I also began to improvise.

Lying in bed, recovering from pneumonia or some other illness, I'd stare at the mobiles pinned to my bedroom ceiling and say whatever I thought—directed to God. I didn't especially think that he was on my ceiling, or even beyond it, but somehow my eyes naturally went upward. At that time, my prayers were usually for my family or asking about the future—would I be able to go to college, for example. Or when I was struggling to breathe or upset about something, I might ask God to help me be calm enough to fill my lungs with air.

Often, too, my prayer might verbally wind down and I would just sit with God, imagining his presence with me even as I was, physically, alone in my room. Far from experiencing the stereotypically angry, punitive, or distant God, those moments of quiet brought me incredible comfort and only made me want to talk to God more.

So I began to view God as a friend. I started to read the Bible and stories of the lives of the saints. This way, I began to learn of the connection between faith and acting on that faith, of living with illness and other trials while having faith, too, and good grace. Of how prayer relates to spiritual growth and personal strength.

At the time, I did not realize I was setting the stage for a lifelong practice of talking with God, let alone developing spiritual muscles and an arsenal of skills that would help me through difficult crises and enhance the happier times of life! As I continued into adulthood, praying daily, I began to realize how essential my time with God was and is, and how blessed the spiritual deep breathing was each time I took the time to enjoy it. Even when I was in the very angry place after that one particularly difficult move, prayer was a haven for me, and a place of tremendous inspiration that, eventually, allowed me to move forward.

Powerful Prayer

Each person prays in a very individual way. For that reason alone, it's nearly impossible to cover all that prayer is or does in one chapter or even a series of books! But there is common ground when we speak of prayer, and this helps us not only understand one another, but enable people of vastly different faith walks, religious persuasions (or none), ages, and life circumstances to unite in prayer around disasters, causes, individuals who are suffering, and other crisis-fraught situations.

One common element of prayer is that when we pray, we get out of our own way and focus on talking with God—and listening attentively to his response.

The practice of prayer also takes us to different and more profound levels the longer we do it. We all start, perhaps, as I did, with pre-established prayers. We reflect on the words, taking them one by one, and let the meaning sink in. As we do this, we think beyond the prayer to more—more about angels, God, life, death, help, and grace.

As we deepen our prayer, spending more time in quiet contemplation, we recognize the hidden treasures within ourselves (very exciting) and face our frailty and faults (very daunting). This is similar to having a long conversation with a trusted friend and, after the superficial phase, finding out exactly what he or she finds that is wonderful about us and what might be improved upon. In this candid level of prayer, we realize that we possess more riches than we previously recognized, but we also cannot avoid our failings, times, and ways in which we could have done better. We trip across our burdens of anger, resentment, and things we hold against others, God, or even ourselves. We realize that we should resolve them so that we can move ahead more closely with God, our friend.

Going deeper still, we become better aware of who we are and of our place in the world. Here, we find more profound peace as we cultivate compassion within ourselves. We find forgiveness. We build spiritual strength. We realize that pain, illness, sorrow, grief, and other physical and emotional challenges can be well-met and handled with the peace and strength we find in praying regularly and deeply, and this realization is proved correct when, through action, we see these things become true. And so, we crave prayer, those precious conversations with God, even more.

The time we spend in prayer helps us build strong spiritual muscles that are more likely to instinctively flex in protective ways when we are faced with a crisis or think that one is imminent. Much like a protective shield, when we call upon God in prayer when we're in trouble, as Michael Bellinder did when he was faced with death, we are summoning the support and calm that we cultivate in our quiet, non-threatened prayerful practice. This is one of the most powerful and wonderful aspects of prayer: Intangible, extremely personal, and fluid, deeply cultivated prayer provides us with the ability to find God in crisis and to shield ourselves from panic.

In my own life, I've felt that surge of prayer, uninvited by me, and seen it answered.

I'd gone for a full year without being diagnosed with lupus. I was very, very sick, but no doctor I saw would run any blood tests or really take my symptoms any more seriously than telling me I was stressed. Finally, I was sitting in one of my doctors' offices at the end of one more frustrating appointment when a prayer popped up in my head.

"Please, Lord, tell me what to ask so I can find answers."

The next thing I knew, I was telling my doctor to run blood tests. She said it wasn't necessary, that there was no possibility that anything serious was wrong with me.

But, that voice in my head popped back up and, this time, I opened my mouth and said, "Humor me. It's my blood. It's my money. Humor me."

Very reluctantly, the doctor wrote out an order for some tests. And within a month, I was sitting with another doctor, a rheumatologist, who was telling me that lupus was trying to kill me!

At the time, I'd never really spoken up to a doctor like that before. I didn't know what lupus was. I didn't really consciously put anything in motion—but I did allow the Spirit, strengthened by all of those years of prayer, to come forward when I certainly needed it most!

Prayer Practice

I really believe there is no right or wrong way to pray. But there are some things we can do to help ourselves benefit more fully from a prayerful activity. We can pray anywhere, but if we are too distracted by our environment, we will not gain great depth in our conversation with God. So if you are just beginning your prayer journey, or if you have particularly deep needs to bring to God in prayer, take your deep spiritual breath to somewhere quiet where you can speak and hear more clearly.

What do you say to God? If you are new to daily prayer, it can help to memorize a few prayers that are starters for you. Those who meditate may develop words, sounds, or phrases that they repeat as they move deeper into their meditative session. A sacred text, such as the Bible, or prayers that have been written by very spiritual men and women are good sources. You might want to write a prayer or two of your own, perhaps one for greeting God in the morning and one for checking in with God in the evening. Rest assured, you do not have to have a degree in theology to write and speak your own prayers!

Like good conversation, good prayer is give and take, speaking and silence, talking and listening. As you verbalize your prayers, leave time and energy for sitting silently, attention inward, and tune your heart and ears in to hearing any whisper from the Spirit, any words from God. Often, God's voice might be so personal to us and come from such a deep place that we cannot fully translate the message into words we might come up with. Even so, God does listen, hear, and respond—in his way and in his time.

Each person will develop his or her own style of prayer, but each prayer and each time we pray will be distinct from all others!

It will feel as if your words are flowing and your soul is being filled with joy, energy, and grace. Other times, it will seem as if all you want to do is cry or sit numbly. Still other times, you might feel as if you are getting nowhere—no answers are coming from God, and your own human head is a tangle of confusion.

Some degree of feeling tangled is, at times, good. After all, as much as God is a friend, he is also *God*, and very much beyond our full comprehension. But sometimes, too, we are our own worst enemy when it comes to good, deep prayer.

Anger with God can throw up a wall that's difficult to get past in prayer. If you harbor resentment against God ("Lord, I am angry with you because you aren't answering me / giving me what I asked for / relieving me from the pain of this situation…") try asking for wisdom instead, which can help turn you from anger toward comfort.

Another impediment to deepening prayer is when we pray with an ulterior motive. Here are some examples of how frustration, hurt, or anger can twist our feelings and words in prayer:

• Misplaced loyalty: "Lord, I know you will take care of them for hurting me (or a loved one)."

• Misplaced gratitude: "Lord, I'm glad the storm wiped them out and spared me. Thank you!"

• Misplaced righteousness: "Lord, you've given me so many gifts, more than others, so I know you'll give me success."

We might have a long list of prayers for other people. Health. Employment. Security. Wisdom. Strength. We lift up worldly concerns, too, asking for safety for people touched by war or disaster. But we might become overly frustrated and tired when our prayer list is so long that we have no energy left for that quiet, profound time just talking and listening to God. It's all right, in fact, it's important to dedicate time in prayer for yourself. This will not only benefit you, but it will also make you more attentive and effective when you pray for others.

Presence of Prayer

We can pray anywhere—and in fact, it is good to bring an awareness of prayer to every aspect of our lives. In this way, it will be more likely that we will utilize prayer for coping if something unexpected occurs.

We can also incorporate prayer into other meditative practices, such as Tai Chi or yoga. Blending prayer with deep breathing can help focus our attention inwardly and is especially good for relaxing into a long stretch of praying. One of my friends told me that, when she has difficulty breathing, she is conscious of breathing in God and breathing out God, and in that way, she feels the spiritual support of a loving Creator all around her, as well as inside.

A simple walk around the block can be a powerful way to pray for your neighborhood and community, as well as for the natural beauty of God's world. This exercise, or any kind of physical exercise, can accompany prayer and build the body's muscles along with the spirit!

In church, prayer sometimes becomes hurried, and we become distracted easily if we haven't left our daily responsibilities or cares outside (or if we're involved with the service, and it seems like a time for work as well as worship). If you are very busy at your church, consider dedicating one Sunday a month to not working at the service, focused on your place and prayer in the pew. Getting to church early can help find quiet in a sacred house of worship, as can spending time afterward in reflection. I like to go to an empty, unfamiliar church at off hours sometimes and sit, pray, and enjoy the silence.

Some people find keeping a prayer journal helpful. They might jot down prayers lifted up and prayers answered, for example, or they might keep a kind of diary of their conversations with God. I kept a prayer and meditation journal when I was first diagnosed with lupus because the disease caused a brain fog that made it difficult to remember what I'd prayed for! Amazingly, that simple, practical journal became my first spirituality-related book, *Peace in the Storm: Meditations on Chronic Pain and Illness*. I'm forever amazed at where God leads when I'm obedient in prayer!

How Do We Know God Answers Prayer?

My diagnosis of lupus has brought me many blessings, but one of the most unexpected ones is that the experience reaffirmed my belief in God. Moreover, it helped me better define (for myself) how I can better discern God's will and, thus, take much of the stress out of daily life.

First, my reaffirmed belief. When I was diagnosed, my first reaction was, "OK, so what medication do I take and when will I get over it?"

Then, I learned that lupus is incurable and that there were (and still are) no medications for it that do anything but sometimes manage some of the symptoms—and most of those medications have horrible side effects. I further learned that scientists still don't know what causes lupus, nor why each patient's disease activity and severity is different. Finally, I learned that I would have to drastically change my lifestyle because of the disease, but even with those changes, I still might, at any time, unexpectedly go into a flare. Without notice. Without doing anything of my own to bring it about.

Sure enough, since then, I have, indeed, lived the life with lupus that

I learned about when I was diagnosed. But far from being discouraged, my belief in God has been reaffirmed. This is because I am living with an incurable, unpredictable, potentially life-threatening illness that has very inadequate treatments and requires extensive lifestyle modifications. I'm *living*!

Science can't cure me. I can't completely stop flares from happening. The disease has damaged organs, precipitated infections, and shows no sign of letting up. But the fact that I am able to write this book alone is witness to God. If it were up to nature or chance, I doubt I'd be here. But I believe I am here because of God.

This belief colors all of my feelings toward any potential crises that may lurk in the future.

All else might be grim and hope seem distant. Pain might be horrible and options limited, if present at all. But God is. And so, in prayer, when I'm bringing a concern or question, I am confident that he will answer.

That answer might not be what I expect or desire. It might not come immediately, and it might not be apparent when it does. But if I'm careful and quiet, if I take the time to listen carefully, I hear a distinct whisper that guides me. And if I reflect attentively, I sense a solid floor of support beneath me as I move from one day to the next and one crisis or period of calm to the next. That floor helps me keep on track; if I deviate from it, if I go one way but should have gone the other, I sense the instability and imbalance in my life almost immediately.

In the Old Testament, God spoke through burning bushes and from clouds high in the sky. He could still do that today, but I think that it's in the whispers we hear and the support we feel that our prayers are answered. All the more reason to dive ever deeper into quiet, profound, and personal prayer.

FAITH IN FOCUS

Our minds can become so cluttered with worries and stress that we forget when God answers our prayers. Bad news and thoughts have a tendency to stick more tenaciously to us than good. One of my dear friends has a wonderful way of reminding herself of when God answers her prayers: She places an empty jar by her front door. Next to the jar is a dish of corn kernels. Each time God answers a prayer, she puts a kernel of corn in the jar. As the jar fills, my friend's heart becomes more full of thanks for answered prayers! Try filling a jar or another vessel with proof of answered prayers. Have faith that what you pray for is heard—and that God does answer!

By ourselves, we might feel totally alone, vulnerable, lost, and panicked. But when we pray, we open the door wide to strengthening the Spirit and inviting God to tackle the problems there with us.

Even those who might not consider themselves people of faith on a daily basis might recognize what I'm talking about. So often, I've heard people who ordinarily would not acknowledge faith say that they prayed at a time of deep pain, or when they felt there was nowhere else to turn. Prayer is a treasure that way: It is always available, just as a supportive, loving God is always available, too. And for anyone, especially for people who are not used to experiencing answers to prayer, prayer can be a life-changing experience that rushes them right into the center of the beauty of being human: the center that is the soul.

CHAPTER EIGHT

What Are You Missing?

"There will always be someone richer, smarter, or more attractive
than you are—but they will never be you!"
—the late Dorothy N., my grandmother

When I was studying to be a translator, one of the most important
things I learned was to recognize when I did not know something.
Only then could I find out what it was I did not know. The worst thing,
especially when it comes to translating sensitive documents, would be
to go ahead with a translation that wasn't right, that was somehow
rushed or inaccurate. Wars and deep wounds have been instigated on
much less than a mistranslated word!

When you are facing a crisis, the lesson of learning to know what
you don't know is applicable, too. If you pull a bag over your head and
rush into the action without taking stock of your resources, you risk
being woefully inadequate or, in the worst case, making the situation
worse. For example, if a relative has a medical crisis and you only rely
on knowledge acquired through hearsay, you risk doing or saying something that could negatively affect that relative's health and well-being.
Likewise, if you were to advise someone on a legal matter without
being a licensed attorney or expert, you would not only risk making a
situation worse, but you could be accused of doing something illegal.

It is natural to want to reach out and help others in trouble, especially
if they are beloved to us. And it is only natural to want to resolve a crisis
of our own as quickly and easily as possible. But we must be realistic

and fully consider our resources, the "what is" of the situation, in order to move ahead. Surprisingly, rather than being a thing of weakness, a gap or deficit in our own resources can become a tremendous asset; we can fill those gaps with people and knowledge that is better, more reliable, and more effective than any we might have ourselves, and thus, we become much stronger overall.

Yes, there is great strength in knowing what we don't know—and then finding out what we need. But first, we must determine what we're lacking.

The Necessary

The construct given to us by St. Francis of Assisi—considering the necessary, then the possible, and then, suddenly, doing the impossible—is a perfect frame for thinking about, determining, and then finding what we might need to tackle a crisis.

First, the necessary:

• *Information and Guidance:* These include legal, medical, theological and other specialized expertise that you might require to handle a crisis. A clergyperson can assist with burial preparations, for example. A lawyer is needed to handle child custody, divorce, and civil proceedings. An appropriate medical professional should be consulted about serious health issues (by this, I mean consulting the correct specialist; not all physicians are equipped to manage care for all medical conditions). An accountant is the best person to sort through complex tax issues. Find these and other experts through your network of friends, church community, high school or college alumni association, or other organization to which you belong.

• *Personal Support:* Any of us in a crisis needs support, and to get this, we have to communicate clearly with our loved ones about what we need from them. If you are in a crisis and feel you are being left to deal with it all by yourself, examine how you have tried to communicate your need for others to help and be supportive. Use your creativity to reframe your requests for help in ways that the other person might better understand. If you still feel left completely alone, expand your request to your clergyperson, the greater church community, doctor, or neighbor. Pray for guidance and direction—God works through others, and we must never give up allowing God to do just that for us!

• *Money and Time:* Oh, there will never be enough of these when a crisis strikes! Although we might feel we are severely lacking in one or both of them, we need not feel that our limited monetary and time resources are inadequate; it's only that they are less than we would like. Help others around you, including any legal, medical, or other experts you enlist, understand your finite resources, and ask them to work with you. Perhaps you can arrange a payment plan for fees, or schedule crisis-related activities creatively so that you do not have to drop family, work, and other responsibilities completely during the time of crisis. Discuss your money and time constraints with your loved ones, ask for their input, and if needed, ask for help. Carefully, and with the assistance of trusted friends and experts, filter offers of assistance, especially from strangers or organizations and businesses that might be suspect; often disreputable people prey upon people floundering financially in a crisis, and you want to do all you can to avoid subjecting yourselves to them.

• *Personal Strength or Will:* Even when others depend upon you, or you are dependent upon yourself, you might feel as if you are simply not strong enough to weather a particular crisis. Perhaps you have been through too many trying times, or perhaps a crisis occurs at a time in your life when you are particularly weak or vulnerable. The truth here is that you have strength, and you do have good will. But maybe you need to refocus your attention so that you, too, realize this and are able to make use of these and other resources.

How, exactly?

The Possible

Excellent resources might be at hand, and we might profess faith and know, intellectually, what we need to do when a crisis occurs. But sometimes, we might ignore or shy away from the most obvious tools we have inside and around us. Sometimes we have to bend our pride, change our lifestyle practices, or dig even deeper into our hearts to unearth, dust off, and benefit from what makes it possible to cope. Some of these hidden treasures are:

• *Humility:* Think you have to do it all in a crisis? Think only you can handle a problem? Are you afraid of admitting you have a problem at all? Whether you are a fiercely strong breadwinner or a brilliant scientist homemaker, there is no shame in turning to others for support, knowledge, and wisdom. Carrying the full weight of a crisis is agonizing and unnecessary. So cultivate humility within so that you can understand what you need to proceed.

• *Humor:* Crises are serious, yes, but humor is a God-given and important tool for coping and should not be overlooked. Find something to laugh about to break up the stress—laugh about, not at, something within the moment or outside of it (a funny picture, cartoon, or joke). Help others to do this, too. Laughter releases hormones that are associated with well-being; when we laugh, we're less likely to panic!

• *Health Habits:* Solid and sustainable healthy habits in diet, exercise, sleep, lifestyle (not smoking, for example), and elsewhere through daily life set us up for better physical support when we face a crisis. And a doctor's guidance can be a true lifesaver during a crisis. Whenever I'm faced with a particularly stressful situation, I include my medical team in the conversation about how to healthfully cope. Putting off health considerations until times are calmer can create more trouble, instead of less.

• *Gratitude:* If you let yourself believe that you have nothing to be thankful for, that life is one string of problems after another, and there is nothing you can do, then you will absolutely overlook valuable resources within yourself or your immediate surroundings. By cultivating within you a regular posture of gratitude, appreciation for all of the good in your life, you can see how much you already have, and how many resources are available to you when trouble comes.

• *Steadfastness:* Crises turn our worlds upside down, but sometimes we let them create so many problems in other aspects of our lives that we wreck more than what the crisis might have. If you feel as if your entire life is lacking stability, consider how you set and maintain boundaries, even during trying times. Take a deep emotional breath and start to reestablish your reliability in your spiritual practices, relationships, workplace, and elsewhere so that when the crisis subsides, you will have intact places and people to return to.

• *History:* Throughout this book, the "Faith in Focus" portions are meant to encourage thought about your past and how you might rely on that for the future. Truly, our past accomplishments inform and inspire us as we face new challenges, even if these are drastically different from the previous ones. Do not forget your history of meeting other crises. Do not forget the strength you found within and the lessons you learned. Remember—and use them.

• *Examples.* If you still believe that you are inadequate to rise to a challenge, consider the examples of other people who have faced and coped with crises and come out of them with resilience and grace. Some of the stories in this book might inspire you and be helpful guides for you, and you undoubtedly know of others. Remember that each of these people is not superhuman or particularly lottery-winning lucky. Rather, these men and women (and some children) are human just as you are, and possess many of the same gifts that you do. If they could weather horrible crises, you can, too.

The Impossible

In the midst of a crisis, it is normal to think we might not ever feel safe, whole, or healed again. The desire to be crisis-free, to have life return to calm, might seem absolutely impossible. Yet, if we persevere in faith, prayer, fellowship and friendship, a singular light emerges.

In December 2014, I was having a very tough time dealing with the possibility of going blind, as well as my usual lupus-related challenges. I was on a high dose of a medication to try to stop what doctors thought was retinal deterioration due to autoimmune antiretinal antibodies. I'd lost vision in both my eyes, but my practical vision was still excellent (an odd occurrence, but then, most of my life with lupus has been a bit odd).

With the busyness of the holidays, and crunch time with deadlines, the underlying stress over whether the medication would work came fully forward as testing indicated there had been further deterioration. My doctors agreed we could try increasing the medication's dosage and then retest in six months, but the tone of that appointment was anything but uplifting. There was a cloud over my head—a great, dark, ominous cloud. One day, I became frustrated with a new toaster oven. Its digital readout and myriad settings seemed more suited for the cockpit of an airplane than my kitchen counter. I started to cry. My mother was comforting, but I retreated to my room, and the tears flowed. There, I opened my Bible, the one I keep on my nightstand that belonged to my brother Casey.

I've read the entire Bible many times, but never before had I focused on this one passage from Sirach. It leapt out at me that day at just the right time and place. The beginning was difficult to read, but as I continued, pure peace enfolded me.

I invite you to read these verses slowly, thoughtfully, breathing gently as you do:

I give you thanks, O God of my father;
  I praise you, O God my savior!
I will make known your name, refuge of my life;
  you have been my helper against my adversaries.
You have saved me from death,
  and kept back my body from the pit.
From the clutches of the nether world you have
    snatched my feet;
  you have delivered me, in your great mercy
From the scourge of a slanderous tongue,
  and from the lips that went over to falsehood;
From the snare of those who watched for my downfall,
  and from the power of those who sought my life;
From many a danger you have saved me,
  from flames that hemmed me in on every side;
From the midst of unremitting fire,
  From the deep belly of the nether world;
From deceiving lips and painters of lies,
  from the arrows of dishonest tongues.
I was at the point of death,
  my soul was nearing the depths of the nether world;
I turned every way, but there was no one to help me.
  I looked for one to sustain me, but could find no one.
But then I remembered the mercies of the LORD,
  his kindness through ages past;
For he saves those who take refuge in him,
  and rescues them from every evil.
So I raised my voice from the very earth,
  from the gates of the nether world, my cry.

I called out: O LORD, you are my father,
    you are my champion and my savior;
Do not abandon me in time of trouble,
    in the midst of storms and dangers.
I will ever praise your name
    and be constant in my prayers to you.
Thereupon the LORD heard my voice,
    he listened to my appeal;
He saved me from evil of every kind
    and preserved me in time of trouble.
For this reason I thank him and I praise him;
    I bless the name of the LORD.
(Sirach 51:1–12)

So often, we think we're missing something, anything, to meet a crisis. Sometimes it seems impossible that we'll move through hard circumstances. And sometimes, the tears flow even if we are strong, resilient, spiritual warriors! But no matter how we are feeling, gratitude, history, humor, and remembrance of these when tied with faith in God, will dry those tears and support us—onward.

CHAPTER NINE

Your Crisis Preparedness Kit

Here in earthquake-prone California we are urged to keep emergency supplies at the ready in the form of an earthquake preparedness kit. Extra food, water, batteries, blankets, and other items we might need if the infrastructure is badly damaged. We're also advised to keep a kit in the car and pack it with similar items as well as car-specific things (flares and a temporary tire, for example) that might come in handy if we're stranded on the road.

A crisis preparedness kit serves much the same purpose as the physical one we might go to if we're involved in a natural disaster or situations such as civil unrest. It, like the one I keep in case of earthquakes, not only contains practical tools and provisions but also gives peace of mind. A robust and ever-stronger crisis preparedness kit can diminish our tendency to panic at the thought of being sunk should serious trouble arise around or inside of our bodies, hearts, or souls.

This book is really a primer for building your personal crisis preparedness kit. In this chapter, you'll find guidelines for what to consider in each section of your kit and how to replenish and grow the contents so that you feel even stronger and better prepared to face any of life's crises. True crisis preparedness begins with you!

You, Yourself, and Life

Crises demand physical, emotional, and spiritual strength, and the more we build those attributes, the better prepared we will be. So, as you start your kit, make one section for:

• Health Assessment and Maintenance: Sometimes we try not to face health issues that we should be dealing with because we are afraid, proud, or too busy to address them. But the more we push them aside, the greater the potential harm. Try to take the mystery off of your overall health situation and work with your doctor to tackle any problems that might undermine your ability to weather a crisis. Establish a good exercise program, encourage yourself and your loved ones to eat healthfully, and take advantage of calm, crisis-free times to build healthful sleep and relaxation habits so that you can rely on them when life is stressful. Write down what you need to do and the progress you make so you can see how effectively you are storing up physical strength.

• Positive Social Supports: If your life is hectic, your social circle might be a bit ragged. Perhaps there are people you love but don't spend time with and others who are more toxic to you, but they seem to wriggle their way into your calendar, crowding out the more positive, true friends. Gently, but consistently, fill the "Social Supports" compartment of your crisis preparedness kit with true, honest, good friends who will be gems for you when crises arise—and for whom you will be a good friend, too. Spend time cultivating these relationships and enjoy the benefit of fortifying your life with such friendships.

• Spiritual Development: No matter where we are on our faith journey, no matter what religion we do or do not practice, our souls benefit from consistent, constant attention and development. Find your preferred way to spend time in quiet and cultivate activities that enhance your spiritual growth (deep breathing, for example). Focus on having more faith in your life and bring that desire for trust into a lively conversation with God that continues. Challenge yourself to persevere in prayer and good spiritual practice, no matter how much society's influence or others might try to persuade you to give up. Listen for

God, feel that solid floor of his support beneath your feet, and crave to go even farther.

• Time Management: We might think we often have no control over our time, but we have more than we imagine. Only, sometimes we automatically agree to have that time usurped, or we spend much of it idly, trying to decide what to do with it! Understand how you use time, observe how you schedule your time, and recognize where you could reclaim more of it, using it for strengthening, enriching life pursuits. Equate time with goodness (it is a great gift) and fill it accordingly.

• Love Who You Are and What You Do: So much of our fear and sense of panic can stem from feelings of inadequacy—we won't be strong enough, rich enough, or popular enough to insulate ourselves from disappointment, hurt, or myriad problems. But there is something very purposeful within you, something that sets you apart from everyone else. When you discover this and bring it forward into who you are, into yourself and others, and into what you do, in work and by witness, life becomes brighter and panic fades. Know what you are, what you know, and what you can do. Love these things, and learn to supplement what you might lack with people who are good and knowledge that is true.

Understanding ourselves is a lifelong process. But the more we grow our physical, emotional, and spiritual lives the more resources we have to carve out paths that are uniquely, strongly, and courageously us!

Nuts and Bolts
Prepare a solid foundation of nuts and bolts of crisis preparedness.

• Legal: When we address practical matters proactively, we take great stress off of the shoulders of our loved ones, and we make sure that our wishes will be respected. So take steps in advance to get a healthcare directive, power of attorney, will, and if necessary, prearrange funeral details. If you have small children, ease your worry about them by legally designating someone to oversee their care should you be unable to do so.

• Financial: Even if we have very few financial resources or live paycheck to paycheck, it is important that we use our God-given minds to learn about how money works and how to use it well. No get rich quick schemes here, but realistic, "what-is" thinking and planning about spending, saving, and giving. When a crisis arises, the emotional and tangible difference between having even a little bit saved versus being already fathoms deep underwater with debt can be immense!

• Safety: The more we equip ourselves with safety knowledge, the more secure we will feel when a crisis hits. This knowledge can be in the form of cardiopulmonary resuscitation (CPR) or first aid training, fire and disaster drills, or an understanding of your area's disaster warning or alert system. Also, examine your home and try to eliminate potential hazards. As we age, what might not have been a hazard in our youth could pose one now, such as storing things on high shelves as we become older when it is more difficult to manage a stepstool.

• Referential: I delight in knowing other people's talents, and sometimes this comes in handy when I'm experiencing a crisis or know someone else who is, and I am always grateful when I can help someone because of expertise I have developed. Doctors, lawyers, accountants, mechanics, pharmacists, clergy—these are valuable resources. So, too, are counselors, friends with excellent senses of humor and calm, first responders, patients who suffer from the same or a similar illness.

• Worldly: Even if we live in a small town in the middle of a corn-field, we need to be aware of our world, constantly updating our knowledge about what is happening near and far so that we can understand what steps we can take to protect ourselves. Observe the world, find where it might affect you and those about whom you care, and create ways to protect yourself from the bad while benefiting from it. A good crisis preparedness kit will change as we gain knowledge, experience, and weather life's storms. It acts as both a diary of what we have done in the past, as well as a template for us to turn to when trouble comes again.

CHAPTER TEN

Light Within and Light Up Ahead

We cannot tell the future, and so we cannot say with certainty what crises might occur in our lives and world tomorrow, next month, or next year. We can be certain that, as long as people populate the earth and are wonderfully and frightfully human, there will undoubtedly be trouble that will adversely impact us, our families, and our communities.

But we can be just as certain that we have a light inside, a spirit that inspires us and others, especially when crises arise. Moreover, each of us has talents, special and unique, that we can bring to bear before and after any of life's challenges. The stronger we allow ourselves to be, the more vigorously we will bring out light and talents to ourselves and others, whenever and wherever hurt may happen.

Although there are serious, negative pressures all around us that work to chip away at our resilience and extinguish the light within, in the beginning and end, how we strengthen ourselves is up to us. And we are not helpless! As you've seen, there are many tools we have been given innately, tools that are free and available immediately to us. There are other resources, too, that can assist us to keep strong and that can provide help in specific ways when we might not have quite the right arsenal ourselves. And there are many others who provide light for us, inspiration and encouragement that show us if these mere mortals were able to overcome sky-high obstacles, we can do so, too.

I've mostly focused in this book on how we can take charge of our physical, emotional, and spiritual lives, and how we can put together our resources, external and internal, so that we are well prepared—and less likely to panic. If we work each day to build up strong bodies, we will be physically able to endure the grueling test of a crisis. If we nurture true friends and strong support systems, nourishing ourselves with what is good while pushing aside what is bad, we will be able to emotionally ride through the ups and downs of life's challenges without being broken. And if we cultivate the Spirit within us, allowing a vibrant conversation with God to blossom and grow through our willingness to forgive and our desire to be grateful, we will never feel alone, unable, or abandoned.

I expect that I will weather many more crises—life was never meant to be easy! But knowing this makes the joy in life, the love and light, so much more precious. Living through hard times makes me understand how strong I can be, and how wonderfully gifted with good people, even strangers, around me who also desire good outcomes from even the hardest challenges.

This is where I think the greatest blessing from crises comes: The good, encouraging, and inspiring people God brings us throughout our lives. People who might be vastly different from us in personality, ethnicity, language, or creed, but who also desire to be more positive than negative, more of a catalyst for light than darkness.

I pray that, as you continue on your life journey, you, too, will be blessed with many good angels on earth, whether fast friends for years or those who move in and out of our days, but leave us with a moment of grace or a bit of warm comfort. Know that these people, too, have gone through crises and understand and have compassion for where you are in yours. And when you recognize just how many of these angels there are and that they recognize you as someone who also brings light, may you feel lifted, supported, loved, and gladdened—and ever ready to reach out to others, too, who need your talents, encouragement, and light.

Through who you uniquely are, through the good talents you build and the Spirit you nurture, through the blessings that are uniquely yours to bring into our troubled world, may you always have faith, and may you never again feel you have to panic!

ACKNOWLEDGMENTS

This book would have been impossible to write without the love and support of my mother and my dear, true friends—Mom, Carolyn and Robert, Fr. Frank, Fr. Michael, Fr. Tom, Beth, Barbara, Nicole, Janet, Judy, Joan, Diana, and so many others. It is to you that I dedicate this book and to you that I say a heart-deep "Thank you!"

I also am very grateful for the generosity of time and wisdom shared by Michael Bellinder, Dr. Wolf Mehling, Dr. Margaret L. Stuber, and Marilyn White. And as always, I appreciate the efforts of my medical team, which saw me through added pain and illness during the writing of this book—many thanks especially to Dr. David Hallegua, Dr. Kathryn Gardner, Rob Thomsen, PT, DPT, and Dr. Jay Schapira.

From the start, the publishing team at Franciscan Media has made me feel like one of the family. My appreciation and great respect go to each brother and sister there, especially Diane Houdek, Mark Lombard, Katie Carroll, Jon Sweeney, Ray Taylor, Angela Glassmeyer, Mark Sullivan, and John Feister.

Finally, I would like to thank the readers of my previous work. When I have been in pain, when lupus has flared, or when crises have arisen and challenged me deeply, your emails, letters, and reposts and tweets have given me extra encouragement, gratitude, and joy. I hope that this book will give you that extra boost, too, and that we can all be light for one another—whether near or far!

NOTES

1. The Younger Pliny, *The Letters of the Younger Pliny*, translated by Betty Radice (Penguin Classics, 1969), 172.
2. For more on the subject, see *The Mayo Clinic Guide to Stress-Free Living* by Amit Sood, MD (Boston: Da Capo, 2013).
3. "Shock," U.S. National Library of Medicine, National Institutes of Health, https://www.nlm.nih.gov/medlineplus/ency/article/000039. htm.
4. University of Texas Counseling and Mental Health Center, *Stress Management and Reduction, Diaphragmatic Breathing*, http://www. cmhc.utexas.edu/stressrecess/Level_Two/breathing.html.
5. W.E. Mehling, K.A. Hamel, M. Acree, N. Byl, F.M. Hecht, "Randomized, Controlled Trial of Breath Therapy for Patients with Chronic Low-Back Pain," *Alternative Therapy Health Medicine*, 11, no. 4 (July–August 2005):44–52.
6. Thomas Aquinas. *Summa Theologica*, "Of the Things That Are Required for Happiness," question 4, article 8, trans. Fathers of the English Dominican Province, (Notre Dame, IN: Benziger, 1948), vol. 2, 608.
7. G.L. Marshall, T. Rue, "Perceived Discrimination and Social Networks among Older African Americans and Caribbean Blacks," *Family Community Health* 35, no. 4 (October–December 2012): 300–11.
8. M. Bernabe, J.M. Botia. "Resilience as a Mediator in Emotional Social Support's Relationship with Occupational Psychology Health in Firefighters," *Journal of Health Psychology* (January 25, 2015), pii: 13591052314566258.
9. A very helpful source on Gandhi's life and spiritual progression is *The Essential Gandhi: An Anthology of His Writings on His Life, Work, and Ideas*, edited by Louis Fischer (New York: Vintage, 1962).
10. Dr. Stuber was quoted as saying this in Marina Dundjerski's article "Faith and Healing," *UCLA Health and David Geffen School of Medicine at UCLA Magazine* (Fall 2013), 16. She repeated these thoughts in an interview I did with her for this book.

11. Aquinas, *Summa Theologica*, question 106, "Of Thankfulness and Gratitude," article 1, vol. 3, 1643.

12. Augustine, *The Confessions of Saint Augustine*, trans. John K. Ryan (New York: Doubleday, 1960), 68.

13. Augustine, 82.

14. For more information about lupus and resources for lupus patients and caregivers, contact the Lupus Foundation of America, www.lupus.org.

15. A movement within the Catholic Church that offers retreats and other means for prayer and spiritual development.

16. Michael Lipka, "5 Facts about Prayer," Pew Research Center, May 6, 2015, www.pewresearch.org/fact-thank/2015/05/06/5-facts-about-prayer/.

17. Press Release from National Center for Complementary and Integrative Health, May 27, 2004, https://nccih.nih.gov/news/2004/052704.htm.

18. Andrew Newberg, MD, and Mark Robert Waldman, *How God Changes Your Brain: Breakthrough Findings from a Leading Neuroscientist* (New York: Ballantine, 2009).

19. K. Wiech, M. Farias, G. Kahane, N. Shackel, W. Tiede, and I. Tracey, "An fMRI Study Measuring Analgesia Enhanced by Religion as a Belief System," *Pain* 4 (August), 147–58, doi:10.1016/j.pain.2008.07.030.

20. I.N. Olver and A. Dutney, "A Randomized, Blinded Study of the Impact of Intercessory Prayer on Spiritual Well-Being in Patients with Cancer," *Alternative Therapies in Health and Medicine* 18, no. 5 (September–October 2012):18–27.

21. K. Jors, A. Bussing, N.C. Hvidt, and K. Bauman, "Personal Prayer in Patients Dealing with Chronic Illness: A Review of the Research Literature," *Evidence Based Complementary Alternative Medicine*, February 26, 2015, doi: 10.1155/2015/927973.

22. Institute for Spirituality and Health at the Texas Medical Center, "fMRI Study on the Effects of Prayer," http://ish-tmc.org/fmri-study-on-the-effects-of-prayer/.

About the Author

Maureen Pratt is an award-winning playwright, journalist and author, as well as a sought-after speaker and patient advocate. Her syndicated column, "Living Well," is distributed through Catholic News Service. Maureen's popular blog, "Good Days...Bad Days with Maureen Pratt" appears on Beliefnet.com. Maureen speaks French and Spanish. She holds a master of fine arts degree in theater arts from the University of California Los Angeles (UCLA) School of Theater, Film, and Television and a BSLA from Georgetown University. Previous books include *Beyond Pain: Job, Jesus, and Joy* and *Peace in the Storm: Meditations on Chronic Pain and Illness*. Her website is www.maureenpratt.com.